THE VIEW FROM
FEDERAL TWIST

THE VIEW FROM
FEDERAL TWIST

A NEW WAY OF THINKING ABOUT GARDENS, NATURE AND OURSELVES

James Golden

filbert press

For Phillip

Throughout the world of gardens there are occasions when something particularly special about a place focuses and shapes both its design and its reception. This may be what was once called the 'sacred', as many early cultures declared. But in a modern world, grown secular and global, this often seems an inappropriate term. Nonetheless, there are places both old and new that call out for some recognition of this special site and its meanings. It may be that a particular place is mysterious, uncanny, even unsettling…

John Dixon Hunt, *A World of Gardens*

Contents

FOREWORD

I found Federal Twist at a moment I desperately needed it. In the fall of 2007, I came across James Golden's exquisite blog. In it he documented his process of clearing the woods and then turning that clearing into one of the most celebrated naturalistic gardens in America. At the time, I was lost professionally. I had just left a job with one of the most iconic garden-makers in the country. I was looking for my own voice, looking for a less contrived aesthetic, and looking for a more authentically ecological design process. James's garden set my head on fire. His soulful photography and poetic writing melted my own self-consciousness. For me, Federal Twist blurred the lines between artifice and nature, native and exotic, plant collecting and place-making. It woke me up.

The story of Federal Twist is remarkable for both the gardener and the garden. James Golden was a white-collar worker in New York who went to the woods of western New Jersey to make a garden. His ambition was great; his site was terrible: mucky wet clay, invasive plants, deer, and the constant pressure of an encroaching forest. Any one of these constraints might be a deal breaker for the rest of us. But James's approach was novel: he turned these stresses into assets. He slowly built paths through the site and then planted into the weeds. James became a student of the great naturalistic designers of Europe and America. Yet he never let this influence give him anxiety. He trusted his own instincts; he observed the way plants grew; he listened to his site.

As a result, Federal Twist was born. It is a garden of great emotional resonance. Part of it is its self-made quality. The uncomplicated gravel paths, dry-stack walls, and artful follies are all details anyone can do. Yet there is a sophistication to the layout that belies its simplicity. Paths follow subtle contours, defining distinct microhabitats throughout. And then there is the planting. It is a garden of big, robust plants. As the heat of summer builds, the planting swells with towering wet meadow species: *Filipendula*, *Eutrochium*, *Silphium*, *Inula*, *Aster*, and *Miscanthus*. While the rest of us fill our gardens with 'tasteful' small and dwarf selections, James prefers massive perennials and grasses. As the sun moves over the garden, these big plants fill with glowing light then fall into deep shadow—a drama with all the quality of baroque tenebrism.

James calls Federal Twist a landscape garden. I think he may be referring to the juxtaposition of scales, both the sweeping clearing in a forest and the many intimate nooks and crannies of the garden. But the phrase 'landscape garden' also is an apt description of the kind of hybrid thinking that makes Federal Twist so special. While often used interchangeably in conversation, the terms landscape and garden represent fundamentally different approaches of place-making. The word landscape derives from the Old English landskip, which refers not to land but to a picture of it. Landscapes are in essence a projection of a mental image onto the land. As a landscape architect myself, I understand that the essence of my discipline is the molding of land to a concept. Yet a garden is different. Gardens are relational. They come alive through time. So for Federal Twist to be a landscape garden represents a fusing of two disciplines: the boldness and vision of the landscape tradition merged with the intimate conversation of gardening.

The true genius of Federal Twist is its half-creation. When staring at the blank canvas of the garden, James made a few light strokes—a path here, a few grasses here—and then waited to see what would happen. Weeds and invasives grew for sure, but so did a latent nature: *Sisyrinchium, Juncus, Onoclea, Scirpus*—key characters of the dramatis personae to come.

To make a mark, then wait. As one who designs landscapes for a living, I find James's wait-and-see approach fascinating. Garden-making is often romanticized, but in reality, it is an act of breaking. Too often, that breaking is of the land itself. Demolish, excavate, terrace, build, import, fill, and then plant. These tools of taming often leave the land unrecognizable. James's process was different, a dialogue in which both existing ecology and human artifice happily comingle.

The need to mark the earth is primal, a revolt against our finitude. Some gardens make that mark with force and flourish, making deep scars that memorialize our existence. But Federal Twist is a different kind of garden. By refusing to break the earth, refusing to make permanent memorials, James instead has created a garden that celebrates the ephemeral. I find this choice profoundly brave and hopeful. More than any other garden I know, Federal Twist is about confronting fear and mortality with a kind of honesty and openness that transforms. This is what brings me back again and again. This is why you need to know this garden.

Thomas Rainer
April 2, 2021

I am Federal Twist. This point was driven home just the

other day. I bought a drone for the sole purpose of seeing my garden from above; I thought it would be a good way to illustrate the complex layout of curving paths in the garden and to monitor and record seasonal changes. On a trial flight over the garden, nearing sunset, I took aerial photographs from far above the sunlit treetops. Later, I took a ground-level photograph looking up toward the house and the tall sycamores (*Platanus occidentalis*) towering above it. The second was very much an image anchored within the garden.

When I put the two images side by side, my reaction was immediate—and astonishing. I felt icy fear. The drone image showed a flat piece of earth totally devoid of feeling, offering no comfort, no warmth, no humanity, no place for me. I felt as if I were seeing with the eyes of an alien being. In contrast, the ground-level photograph held me firmly within the garden; it gave me a place to be, a protected place under trees; it made me a part of the landscape. I felt comforted, and a sense of belonging.

I realize that such powerful feelings are not rational. I had them, nonetheless. Emotions are not controlled by the rational mind. If they were, we wouldn't have so many psychotherapists and psychiatrists, or so many drugs for modulating mood. It is true that I first used the drone in the spring of 2020, during a pandemic, in a time of great social disruption and isolation, so my general anxiety may have intensified my reaction—but my life and emotions are closely bound with this place I call my garden. I understand physics well enough to know that my physical body intersects with the garden, interacts with the garden, responds to the garden in some kind of mutual way. I 'live' the garden every day. I am Federal Twist.

I'll tell you another story. A few years ago, I went to a garden conference in Lund, Sweden. On the way, I stopped over to visit a friend in London, then we both embarked on the short trip to Lund. While we were standing in line at Gatwick to board the aircraft, a travelling companion spoke my name out loud—

'James'. A young woman standing nearby, whom I had never seen before, overheard this and turned and asked me, 'Are you Federal Twist?' This wasn't entirely coincidence—we were all boarding an airplane bound for Copenhagen, en route to a landscape conference in Lund, so we were in a preselected group. I'd been publishing a blog called *View from Federal Twist* for many years, but still, I was astonished that a stranger would connect my given name with the words 'Federal Twist'. My first thought was to ask myself if I had unintentionally become a brand. But no, I realized like never before that, in some real way, I am my garden.

Federal Twist exists only because I create it from day to day. When I die, it will cease to exist. We are one. This isn't a new concept for me, but these two episodes—being identified with Federal Twist while boarding an airplane in another country, and seeing the garden from those two dramatically contrasting perspectives—have driven that awareness home.

And I have a third story, which took place well before the first two. Several years ago, Susan Cohan, a garden-designer friend, drove me to Pleasant Run Nursery to introduce me to the place. She had been encouraging me to join Instagram, but I had had no interest in it, thinking the app was boring and self-indulgent. On this occasion I finally agreed, just as we were about to go into the nursery office, and she said, 'I'll show you how to join right now. What name do you want to use? Think of a name, quick.' I was on the spot. Without stopping to think, I said 'i-m-f-e-d-e-r-a-l-t-w-i-s-t' and that was that. I've been imfederaltwist for several years now.

Last summer I was fortunate enough to spend time with Piet Oudolf in his garden at Hummelo. My friend Giacomo and I had taken a long weekend to visit gardens along the Dutch and German border, and after touring Piet's studio and garden we sat down at a large table near the house. The day was sunny, cool, and breezy—just the kind of day you'd want for visiting Hummelo. Giacomo wandered off to take a photograph, leaving Piet and me alone for a while, and the

LEFT While the view from above can clearly show structure and other garden features not visible in any other way, it is essentially an alien way of looking at a garden.

conversation turned to our age, which is about the same. Piet had been reminiscing about his past and how his life had evolved from a period when he had no idea what he wanted to do, until he discovered his love of plants, and he described how the pieces had fallen into place. I had been thinking how lucky Piet was to have been born just as World War II was coming to an end, because he otherwise might have lived in a time of Nazi occupation. And then I realized I was lucky too, being born just a few days before Hitler died. I said I felt we were both fortunate to have lived in a long period of relative peace and prosperity, at least in our parts of the world, where we could make our own ways and find fulfilling lives. We had both lived 'the good life', in fact privileged lives, in this peaceful interlude between the war and the present time. Piet agreed, in his reserved yet warm Dutch way. I remember a moment of silence. And, though we didn't mention this—it was obvious and so very important—we both live with, and in, our gardens.

I came to gardening late, when I started thinking about retirement—not as some practical way to keep myself busy, but in a much more thoughtful and intentional way. I asked myself where I wanted to be in the world, and I wasn't thinking about physical place. My meaning was far more metaphysical. I wanted to live in a garden, live a garden, in fact, to be a garden.

Could I ask for more?

LEFT Two sycamores on the terrace will probably remain long after my garden has vanished.

OVERLEAF This view of the house, seen from deep inside the garden, creates a feeling of intimacy and belonging, totally different from the aerial perspective.

FROM
A
RIDGE
ABOVE
THE
DELAWARE

I do not know which to prefer,
The beauty of inflections
Or the beauty of innuendoes,
The blackbird whistling
Or just after.

Wallace Stevens, *Thirteen Ways of Looking at a Blackbird*

From a ridge high above the Delaware River, in a wooded area of several thousand acres—fortunately preserved by a confluence of unique geology and relative inaccessibility to commuters—a picturesque landscape, often compared to New England, extends outward into a broken plain and rolling hills. It is a tranquil place, with occasional distant views down to the river, a few surviving covered wooden bridges, several small villages quaintly still called 'hamlets', and canals along both sides of the river.

   This was to be our new home and the place for my garden.

Forest and wilderness

In the northeastern United States, the natural state of the landscape is forest. Though now greatly diminished from the immense and threatening landscape the first Europeans found when they arrived on this continent, that original forest created the myth of wilderness that has become a defining aspect of our culture. In *Where the Sky Began: Land of the Tallgrass Prairie*, John Madson imagines the great mythic wilderness the first European settlers—my ancestors among them—encountered on arrival in what they chose to call the New World:

One of the first things that the new colonists must have known,
as anchor chains rumbled down through hawseholes, was that they
had never really seen trees before . . . they had seen nothing to compare
with this wall of forest that rose behind the coast of America . . .
a limitless wilderness of trees, the infinite and forbidding sweep of
forest that extended from the portals of the New World as far west
as any man knew, and beyond, the greatest forest that western man
had seen during the Christian era.

Today it is said that 'wilderness' itself is a myth, that the Native Americans 'gardened' the great forests in a way Europeans couldn't even see, and certainly could not understand. But today Native Americans do not garden the forest. They were killed or moved out of the way long ago. The great wilderness forests no longer exist, except for relatively tiny bits scattered across the continent, yet even as a remnant, the forest is large and aggressive and what remains will retake

BELOW Looking up at the forest on a rock ledge.

THE VIEW FROM FEDERAL TWIST

any open space. Signs of the past quickly fade. The land is a palimpsest, revealing more recent events with some clarity, but earlier layers of time become more and more difficult to read . . . yet something of the past lingers: atmosphere, character, like the misty edge of memory, coloring the consciousness of any who seek to know it.

Local history is rich, but much of it seems elusive and transitory. The Native Americans of this place, the Lenni Lenape, who lived here for centuries before European settlers arrived, left scattered archaeological remains as the only sign of their existence. Thousands of Irish immigrant laborers who dug canals along the Delaware River in the 1830s using only hand tools have left no mark of their presence, though their memory may linger in the name Federal Twist. No one knows where the name came from, but one of the most credible stories is that the Irish canal workmen had a favorite brand of chewing tobacco named 'Federal Twist'. Chewing tobacco is still sometimes produced in twisted strands.

The first military success in the American Revolution, Washington's crossing of the Delaware on Christmas night in 1776, occurred just a few miles downriver and though that event is ever-present in the local and national consciousness, the fact and meaning of the crossing has faded into a mythic blur. As context for the garden, however, radical events occurring as I write this in autumn 2020—like a clarion call—have suddenly brought the relevance of Washington and the origins of the American republic to the forefront of thought . . . even to thinking about the garden. The first president, Washington—long called 'father of our country'—

who refused a second term for the good of the new country, fearing the people would want to make him king—is a reminder of many things that have gone wrong and that have made the future not just uncertain but even fearful. It has given Washington a new relevance, even in my modest garden.

What I mean is that history and current affairs can't *not* be necessary context for the garden. The same was true in 18th-century England, when many wealthy and politically powerful landowners made their gardens emblems of their political alliances and support. I have no monuments, busts, temples or engraved plaques of individuals I admire, but what I do have is a garden with a point of view and a way of asking to be seen. I hope there's meaning enough in that and, in some way, relevance to life today.

As the area's forests are silent about what happened here, the land itself is complicit in erasing the past. The very geology of the place suggests transience and melancholy. Because the soil is underlain by rock, trees tend to root shallowly and easily fall over, leaving the forest littered with dead and rotting wood, a mark of decay . . . but a decay that brings new life, for the place is intensely green and enfolds you. Standing dead wood and fallen wood are a bounty for insects and wildlife. Every niche of ground that is bare quickly becomes home to germinating seed as new openings in the tree canopy allow light to spark new growth.

The setting

When we moved to a mid-century house overlooking the woods, I knew only a naturalistic garden would suit the place. With a long, low profile, deep overhanging eves, generous use of wood, an unobtrusive, simple, temple-like structure designed to leave a light footprint on the landscape—all suggestive of a Japanese-influenced aesthetic—the house would set an informal, wildish style for the garden. Even the road name, intriguing because of its unknown origin, added a hint of mystery, as did the location, hidden amid woodland cloaking the hilltops above the Delaware.

On a first visit with the real estate agent, as I looked out through a wall of windows across the back of the house, the view gave me pause. I saw below an unkempt wood of eastern red cedar (*Juniperus virginiana*)—a tangle of vines, trees and dangling, dead limbs. Not promising for a garden, I thought. Looking back, my decision to make a garden here seems not entirely rational. I still don't fully understand my acceptance of this very un-gardenlike place as my garden destiny (I wouldn't make another). I do know it had much to do with the house, which clearly would be integral to the garden. The building had an intimate relationship with the place, even in its unkempt state.

I was quite taken with that rather magical idea of this house set amid a garden, and I decided to accept it all—the good with the bad. It led me to create a garden totally different from anything I'd imagined.

LEFT Federal Twist Road is not well known. It's hidden in the woods above the Delaware and is only four miles long.

BELOW I accepted a very ungarden-like place as my garden destiny.

A
CLEARING
IN
THE
WOODS

It is an inftrument with which
to confront the cosmos.

Gaston Bachelard, *The Poetics of Space*

I had planned to have a garden regardless of where we settled. Originally, precedence was to go to finding land good for a garden; the choice of house was to be secondary. But the house we found changed our priorities. It was small, extremely well-designed for living, creatively constructed of simple, ready-to-hand materials, with many aesthetic and practical touches that we took delight in: floor-to-ceiling glass with views out all around; unique design touches and detailed craftsmanship; Modernist use of mahogany paneling, making a kind of brown and white Mondrian effect inside; an intimate entrance space that creates a feeling of anticipation, as you catch brief glimpses into the interior and then on through to the garden on the far side, so that coming into the house is a bit like a ritual and an adventure; a large stone fireplace; and skylights for passive lighting. After we first moved in, I said to Phillip, my husband, 'I feel like I'm living inside a harpsichord.' This was the effect of the mahogany paneling and the light, I think; the design of the house was like a metaphor for music.

Outside was another story.

Constraints and opportunities

Surrounding the house was a monoculture of first-growth eastern red cedar (*Juniperus virginiana*) mixed with invasive multiflora rose, vines, and weeds. On further investigation, I confirmed that the soil was heavy clay, and very wet. These conditions would severely constrain the range of plants I could grow.

When spring arrived, I hired a tree removal company to cut down about 70 junipers, then had the landscape mowed to clear the remaining debris. That was

LEFT Phillip rejoicing on the terrace after we completed the purchase in 2004.

BELOW Heavy snows during our first winter gave me several months to watch and observe the land.

the extent of site preparation. I did find something of value in what the landscape had to give. This woody ruin had character and atmosphere, and I could see the potential for a kind of Picturesque beauty, even meaning, in a crooked dead tree and cloud of yellow leaves. By this time, having looked at magnificent photographs of Piet Oudolf's dying gardens, I had learned to appreciate beauty in decay and death.

We moved in just before the worst of winter, on 1 January 2005, so a delay was necessary until the arrival of spring. The timing was fortunate; it forced me to move slowly, to study the landscape in winter, to begin unravelling the story of the place.

Making a clearing in the woods

Over that first winter I waited, anxious to get the junipers cut and make a clearing to let in light. It was a snowy winter and rather pretty (snow hides a lot). We didn't have a deer exclusion fence then, so I could wander far out into the woods on adjacent land, look back toward the house in its snowy scene, and imagine what the garden could be with all that space available to me. I was standing on preserved land I didn't own; although I couldn't cultivate it, the land would remain forever green, so I could 'borrow' its expansiveness for my garden. I would have to garden a clearing in the woods—a much smaller space—and rely on the surrounding forest to give the garden breathing room.

A clearing in the woods is an archetypal American landscape that came into common use in the 18th and 19th centuries. Open sightlines near the house were needed for security and protection. Such isolated landscapes are still popular for the seclusion they offer. It's a richly symbolic landscape type with deep emotional and historical associations, not just in the United States but also elsewhere; the clearing in the woods is ubiquitous in literature, legends, and stories in many cultures going back to ancient times. Nevertheless, it has become a particularly American landscape, not because the type doesn't exist elsewhere in the world, but simply because our country—in spite of our ravenous culture of suburban development—has many forested areas left, certainly in comparison to Europe.

You might think spatial constraints would limit gardening possibilities. Over the past 15 years, I learned that isn't necessarily so; a woodland clearing offers surprisingly broad capabilities for play of the imagination.

The clearing gives a sense of protection. You are closed off, at least visually, from intruders. This provides a sense of seclusion and comfort during the day and in good weather. But at night you may feel isolated, alone, vulnerable, and unprotected—a feeling I've frequently experienced in my own garden. Such feelings, when used to intensify emotion, can deepen the experience of the garden. You just have to allow that gardens are not all sweetness and light; they also may have a darker side. As in Giorgio Bassani's novel *The Garden of the Finzi-Continis* and Vittorio De Sica's great film of the same name, they can be places of great sadness, anguish, and fear even in the midst of joy.

Such solitary settings are rather common in films and fiction; they easily evoke strong moods and are effective settings for many different kinds of stories. You don't have to look far to find emotional linkages to literary, folk, or past cultural uses: a formal council of Native Americans, a classic American outdoor worship service on a Sunday morning, a happy family picnic, a celebration—or darker stories of a gathering of witches in the night, a meeting place for slaves planning escape, a lynching; any number of secret ceremonies or emotion-laden events come immediately to mind. But such scenes don't need to be specifically referenced. Unless that's the intent—as Ian Hamilton Finlay used the French Revolution and even specific individuals in his garden at Little Sparta in Scotland—my preference is to leave ambiguous hints and suggestions, and let details be heard only as indistinct whispers.

The clearing in the woods is also a classic prospect-refuge setting because it meets the need for both a view out (prospect) and for safety (refuge). The trees and shrubs bordering the open clearing create this environment, which human beings (and many other animals) find so desirable. The house is a refuge looking out onto the sunlit garden, as is the view out from the shade of the woodland garden into the prairie, or the views from any number of quieter niche areas you can retreat to. Many of the chiaroscuro lighting effects to be found in the clearing are also textbook examples of views into light from dark, shady places; they embody the very idea of prospect and refuge.

RIGHT As night arrives, the garden becomes mysterious and even a bit frightening.

A clearing also borrows views into the surrounding woods. While these borrowed views are mostly impressionistic and serve primarily to extend the garden spatially into the surrounding greenness, creating a sense of a more expansive landscape, there are also opportunities for unexpected, and delightful, views out through the complex interstices and apertures formed by tree limbs and plants. And in winter, when the trees are bare, you can see deeply into the

surrounding woods, and even through the woods across the valley of the Lockatong Creek to rounded hilltops on the other side.

Light is another distinctive quality of this landscape. All light is mediated by the geometry of the setting, and here, almost all direct light comes from above, from a sharply defined opening to the sky. The bright midday light can be harsh, so this time is best used for sitting or working in shaded spots—thus the need to provide such areas in which to linger, preferably with a view from protective shade into a sunny area (prospect and refuge again). However, the most emotionally affective lighting comes when the sun is low. Early and late in the day, sunlight pierces through the foliage and creates stunning spotlighting and backlighting effects at all times of the year, even when the foliage is dense.

Fog, snow, and ice can be extraordinary mediators of light, and are especially significant in a spatially limited setting. Snow and ice can be slow and peaceful or stormy and dramatic; it's a bit of a magic trick, and it happens when it happens. Fog is soft and makes objects indistinct, blurring outlines, amplifying colors with an almost painful beauty in autumn. It is the weather condition *par excellence* for

THE VIEW FROM FEDERAL TWIST

Romantic scenes. Fog, with morning sunlight and a brown or golden autumn setting of dying plants and skeletons of trees, can be sublime in the sense Edmund Burke defined it—as both extraordinarily beautiful and threatening in its power. Dark clouds, too, can have a similar effect, under certain light conditions, looming above the oculus of the woodland clearing with stirring emotional force and simultaneous threat. Indeed, light and weather in all their forms are fundamental components of of the garden, not just changing conditions in which the garden exists. Joseph Addison recognized the importance of sensory response in garden design early on: 'why has Providence given it [the material world] a Power of producing in us such imaginary Qualities, as Tastes and Colours, Sounds and

LEFT The emotional pall of dark, broken clouds and dim light.

ABOVE Fog darkens the inula skeletons almost to black and makes the grasses glow.

RIGHT Autumn colors of plants along a pathway backlit by a very low sun—a fantasia of dark line and color. Joseph Addison probably would not have appreciated this naturalistic aesthetic, but he certainly would have understood the importance of the human body's ability to delight in sensory input from the environment.

Smells, Heat and Cold, but that Man … might have his Mind cheared and delighted with agreeable Sensations?' Another remarkable characteristic of a clearing in the woods is the potential for the illusion of immensity in a small space. If tall trees mark the border of the clearing, they will guide the eye skyward, drawing attention to the unbounded space above. And if the clearing at the base

of those trees is relatively open, and especially if there is large foliage in the foreground, through a trick of light and relative scale, the clearing can evoke the kind of large open space you might see in some 18th-century landscape garden. This feeling of immensity constrained can almost take your breath away. Fortunately, the house faces the rising sun, and in autumn, such illusory effects

occur frequently as the low sun rises behind the tall trees.

A clearing can be a place for intensely personal reverie. For years, usually in the low light of twilight, I've had a recurrent fantasy of seeing the garden as if underwater. The clearing is like a cove at the edge of the sea, and the experience of watching the plants swell, in my imagination brushing against one another as darkness rolls in, feels almost a bodily encounter. If the plants sway in a breeze, the breeze is water in motion. The feeling goes beyond sight, smell, hearing, or touch and is more an all-encompassing, bodily sensation. Just yesterday, I was looking out a window where a *Cotinus* 'Grace' has grown swiftly into a great ball of iridescent color surrounded by ligularia, inula, grasses, and spikes of eupatorium, and I imagined that the plants were rising like a sea tide flowing in. At this time of rapid growth, the garden can be felt inside the body; I experience the plants' slow, incessant expansion in a kinesthetic way, almost physically merging with them. In twilight the plant forms may take on imaginary sea shapes, the round, feathery miscanthus becoming a giant sea anemone, rising spires of silphium and inula looming as mysterious sea towers; the whole garden, a sea floor swaying slowly in darkness.

PREVIOUS PAGE Looking toward the sunrise from the terrace of the house, the tall trees and chiaroscuro effects of the light create a sense of immensity even in the relatively small space of my garden. The garden itself is mostly invisible in the dark shadows below.

BELOW In twilight the plant forms may take on imaginary sea shapes, the garden appears as if underwater, a fantasy of the plants rising like a sea tide flowing in, felt inside the body. This is the entrance garden at twilight.

Atmosphere and mood

The German language has a word encompassing a whole range of phenomena related to atmosphere, mood, and feeling that we lack in English; we have no single word that denotes the same range of related meanings. The word is *Stimmung*, variously translated as atmosphere, climate, spirit, mood, feeling; but it also refers to *Stimme*, meaning voice, and to *stimmen*, the tuning of a musical instrument, and by extension 'to be right'. I've recently seen the word translated as 'vibe'.

We may say a garden is 'in tune' with nature but that leaves so much out. *Stimmung* names a broad range of potential feelings, moods, and responses.

What it names is the point of my garden.

When I try to express this, I feel my sentences break apart, become fragments; I point to meanings as meanings dissolve into separate words; I say 'in tune' but that leaves out the sense of 'mood' or 'atmosphere' or some other aspect of intended meaning. I wrote about this expressive difficulty in my blog several years ago. It is mostly a quote directly from Hans Ulrich Gumbrecht, Albert Guérard Professor Emeritus in Literature at Stanford University:

View from Federal Twist
Atmosphere in the Dying Garden
November 19, 2014

I've been reading about atmosphere and mood, but I'm not sure it's possible to put a name to what I feel in the garden. Perhaps it's too personal, perhaps it lives in the body and can't be described in words. . . The text, from Hans Gumbrecht's *Atmosphere, Mood, Stimmung*, focuses on the German word *Stimmung*:

'To gain awareness and appreciation of the different significations and shades of meaning that *Stimmung* conjures up, it is useful to look at the various clusters of words that translate the term into other languages. English offers "mood" and "climate." "Mood" stands for an inner feeling so private it cannot be precisely circumscribed. "Climate," on the other hand, refers to something objective that surrounds people and exercises a physical influence. Only in German does the word connect with *Stimme* and *stimmen*. The first means "voice," and the second "to tune an instrument"; by extension, *stimmen* also means "to be correct." As the tuning of an instrument suggests, specific moods and atmospheres are experienced on a continuum, like musical scales . . .

'I am most interested in the component of meaning that connects *Stimmung* with music and the hearing of sounds. As is well known, we do not hear with our inner and outer ear alone. Hearing is a complex form of behavior that involves the entire body. Skin and haptic modalities of perception play an important role. Every tone we perceive is, of course, a form of physical reality (if an invisible one) that "happens" to our body and, at the same time, "surrounds" it . . .

'Toni Morrison once described the phenomenon with the apt paradox of "being touched as if from inside." She was interested, I imagine, in an experience familiar to everyone: that atmospheres and moods, as the slightest of encounters between our bodies and material surroundings, also affect our psyche.'

'Being touched as if from inside', as Toni Morrison described it—internal experience is physical reality. Your experience in the garden is both in your body and in the garden. This isn't magical thinking; it's reality. It's a part of what we've called spirit of place (*genius loci*) for centuries.

I'm saying the spirit of a place is as real as any plant or physical object in the garden.

Greenness and wildness

Today, when you first enter, before you've had time to explore and see what is garden and what is not, your first impression is not of a garden but of an all-encompassing greenness. The border between garden and surrounding wood is completely transparent—not literally transparent but the green inside blends

THE VIEW FROM FEDERAL TWIST

with the green outside, creating the illusion of transparency—so you see them as one. This is the classic garden technique of using 'borrowed landscape' though in this case what is borrowed is minimal—green space and trees, not distant views. The expansive green also suggests the possibility of wildness.

Although little that is really wild exists here today, I want the garden to be linked with the *idea* of wildness, to evoke a sense of something intangible, unknown, unseen, and perhaps only heard or imagined. In pursuit of that idea of wildness, I kept the ecology of the place as it was, at least to the extent I could, preserved hints of past wildness, did not 'improve' the soil or change drainage patterns. I kept rotting wood and tree snags for atmospheric effect and value to wildlife, and I retained many indigenous plants.

Keeping physical references to wildness appears to work. Visitors seem to experience the garden as 'wild'. With the feeling of wildness, I also want to suggest vulnerability. If you are sitting alone in the garden late on a summer afternoon, for example, you may hear sounds of the wild . . . perhaps coyotes barking in the distance and, though coyotes don't normally attack people, the mere potential of danger awakens the senses, creates an alertness that focuses the mind in the moment.

This isn't to say I want my garden to frighten you if you visit; just that a bit of dis-ease can at times be useful in stimulating the senses and awakening you to the garden's atmosphere.

Finding the spirit of the place

The space a garden is to occupy may seem to be empty and devoid of any desirable characteristics, but that is a nearly impossible condition. Any space, whether neglected or cared for, is charged with possibilities. In most cases, there will be a lot to sort through. Dan Pearson, the noted British garden designer, calls this process 'reading the land'.

Spirit of place comes from the nature of the place itself, for no 'space' is completely neutral. Something is there—trees, swamp, rock, breeze, fragrance, odor, fog, a glint of sunlight, even emptiness itself, absence—that suggests mood or atmosphere, a glimmer of memory, some sort of character. Even in a small city garden, you will find suggestions of place-specific character. In attached row houses, for example, the uniform backs of the houses, often an extensive brick wall punctuated by windows, suggest a presence that might be interpreted in various ways—as protective bulwark against the cacophony of city life, as a kind of memorial reminder of past lives seen through windows in those houses, as a frame for the sky above. Or the existing trees and vegetation behind the houses may suggest a mood or indicate a planting style.

The intangible aspects of place—feeling and emotion, smell, light and dark, sound, fog, rain, wind, snow, warmth, cold—exist without human perception. Can meaning happen only when a human being enters the picture, and one may say, 'I feel cold', 'This autumn fog makes me feel melancholy', or 'Yes, that sunset does remind me of a painting by Caspar David Friedrich'? Without consciousness experiencing the garden, can such words as atmosphere, mood, emotion become relevant to sense of place? Perhaps it doesn't matter that we can't answer these questions, though they nevertheless intrigue.

BELOW The land, though rough and derelict, with heavy clay soil and far too much water, nevertheless suggested a strong character. By accepting it as it was, I was agreeing to make a garden that was informal, naturalistic, ecological, melancholy at times, mysterious, a bit chaotic, wandering rather than direct, with many curves and few straight lines.

I set out to explore the capabilities of the future garden space (in the sense that Capability Brown got his name by identifying and amplifying the 'capabilities' of landscapes). When I first set eyes on the land, the 'raw' landscape strongly suggested an ecology, a style, emotions, and moods (*Stimmung*) the garden might share. By accepting what was given—neglected woods, weeds, heavy clay soil, and too much water—I was agreeing to make a garden that was informal, naturalistic, ecological, melancholy at times, mysterious, a bit chaotic, wandering rather than direct, probably with many curves and few straight lines. I also was agreeing to limit myself to a plant palette dictated by the difficult soil. Such constraints would certainly affect the physical appearance of the garden—though I didn't know how at the time—and flow from 'spirit of place'.

I should clarify my use of the words *space* and *place*. *Space* is simply physical space. It has dimensions and exists in time. *Place* is space given meaning. Place, in this sense, can transcend time and distance, through human memory and consciousness, and possibly in other ways.

It is helpful to recognize the different meanings of the word *place*, at least as I'll be using it. On a regional scale, *place* is the broader landscape, culture, ecology, geology, soils, and climate, including rainfall and surface water, temperature extremes, seasonality, and characteristic weather patterns. How is the region defined? By predominant geographical features, such as the Delaware River Valley, or by political or administrative boundaries, transportation corridors, or by some other means? Is the region predominantly rural or urban? As to the people—who are they, what do they do, where do they live, what do they think, how do they move about? What is the history of the region and its cultural past?

Looking at the local area closer to the vicinity of the garden, place isn't only location. It encompasses salient characteristics of the local area and its culture and history. (What is the character of the area? If agricultural, what crops were grown there? If wooded, what is the history of the land? Is it second growth? Third? What is the character of the landscape as it exists? Are there lakes, rivers, or water courses? How was the land used? What remains of past uses? Were there previous occupants or users of the land nearby and, if so, when, and what did they do there? Can these questions even be answered?)

Taking a much closer and more detailed look at the place of the garden itself, the clearing in the woods, you can ask essential questions about landscape character, size, shape, terrain, notable features, habitat, hydrology, wet and dry areas, soil types. Are there potential physical dangers or environmental threats that can't be addressed at reasonable cost? What are the detailed characteristics of the place? Is there a house? When was it built? By whom? What is the style and how does it sit in the landscape? Is there infrastructure and, if so, what? Was there a garden or yard in the past? What is the character of the site as it exists? What is the drainage and hydrology? How was the land used? What remains of past uses? Were there previous occupants or users of the land and, if so, when, and what did they do there?

So how do all of these capabilities and attributes of the landscape come together in the human impulse to make space into place? I think you look first for emotional connections and imagine a future there. You make it yours. You give it meaning.

Returning home

Returning to the specific site of my garden, the center of 'place' is the house. To keep the house dry, the architect elevated the structure about 12ft (3.6m) above the surrounding land. On the side facing the woods, a long wall of windows looks out, across a slate-paved terrace, onto the area where the garden would be. Three large American sycamores (*Platanus occidentalis*), planted when the house was completed in 1965, provide shade. They also are a major feature of the garden, rising high above the low-slung house, vertically expanding the perceived space of the clearing.

When I began to design the garden, the elevated position of the house proved to be extremely important and a distinguishing characteristic of the clearing in the woods. I realized the place was telling me the house and the raised plinth it rested on were the conceptual center of the garden. While it was raised up for a very practical reason, it also seemed to me strongly symbolic. The resemblance to an altar didn't escape me.

As I removed trees, cleared the shrub layer of multiflora roses and vines, and opened the land to light, I knew that practical ecological concerns would be intrinsic to achieving aesthetic goals. From the start, I was committed to using the site ecology essentially unchanged and saw the virtue of accepting site constraints to evoke mood and atmosphere (*Stimmung*). My ultimate goal would be to transform a derelict, waterlogged woodland into a garden of emotional power. I wanted to layer the new into the old, making a kind of amalgam of past and present, to weave together the existing ecology with the new.

At the start, the land appeared to offer only hardship, but by forcing me to adapt, experiment, develop an appropriate palette of plants, and learn new management techniques, the place led me to transform constraints into opportunities, ultimately resulting in a garden of singular character.

As I observed indigenous plants for clues to what might grow well in this place, the one absolutely clear indicator, growing with great vigor, was *Equisetum arvense* (horsetail or marestail), which likes wet conditions. While its thriving presence wasn't a great help as a guide to ecology (I already knew my soil conditions), the plant itself had a beautiful and intricate structure and, spreading in feathery masses across the ground, seemed a symbol of endurance. Strange as it may be to those who think of it as one of the ultimate evil weeds, its intricate, ordered structure and wild abundance was an early hint of what my garden might become.

ACCEPTING
WHAT
EXISTS

Asked how he imagines the garden of the future, Gilles Clément answered, 'I believe that gardens will either be ecological, or they won't exist, the opposite is unimaginable.'

Alessandro Rocca (ed.), *Planetary Gardens: The Landscape Architecture of Gilles Clément*

When I made the decision to accept 'what exists'—the wet clay soil and the rough, coarse nature of the place—I understood that I would be making an ecological garden, and I would have to develop the practical skills and knowledge needed to do that.

'What exists' was an awful site for a traditional garden; most people would have seen the constraints of the site as reason enough not even to try. However, so much land in our world has been used and abandoned, left wasted, I wanted to use it as found, not to change its essential character, but simply to help it be a better version of itself. I believe that by paying attention, and taking appropriate action, you can make a garden almost anywhere.

Since I began my project, or my experiment I should say, I have seen what extraordinary things can result from attention and care. The Jac. P. Thijssepark in Amsteelveen in the Netherlands is an exemplary model for tending a garden closely tied to its ecology. Thijssepark was originally developed several decades ago and has become quite well known in the gardening world as probably the best of several *heemparks* (home parks) in the Netherlands. (And though it is probably the epitome of the ecological garden, it is a created ecology, having been made on land formerly under water.) It is an attentively managed place, cared for by gardeners familiar with the ecological requirements of the species living there

OPPOSITE We cut many trees to open space in the first spring and the tree removal equipment left deep scars. Looking at these muddy ruts, I quickly understood my garden would have to be an ecological one. Plant selections would have to survive in an ecology of heavy, wet clay and in a temperature range appropriate to my zone 6b.

LEFT Wherever water collects on our impermeable clay, there will be frogs—yet another indicator of the ecology.

and with the subtleties of ecologically informed management. I had read about the Thijssepark long before I visited it, and though my garden is vastly different from Thijssepark in its plant composition and style, its story helped me better understand what I was undertaking—the need for attention to what happens day by day in the garden, and the ability to respond quickly as things change. I understood, for example, that the garden couldn't be managed on a schedule. I had to pay attention and take action in the moment. I've adopted James Hitchmough's plain-spoken appeal to 'respond creatively to what is in front of you'.

The shade, the heavy clay, the rocks, the wet soil, the puddles, the decay all spoke of an ecology, though I couldn't give it a name, and that ecology would be fundamental to giving meaning and character to my garden, and to making the most of what was offered by the place. These conditions are embedded in the natural landscape, and my responses to the constraints, as presented to me, would make the garden unique, and give it unique character. Acceptance, I realized, would be the key to creating a garden which felt 'right' in its place.

Much of my garden is a wet prairie, created from a mixture of native and non-native grasses and perennials, exaggerated and amplified through use of large American prairie plants, miscanthus from Japan, and a tall Dr. Seussian daisy from the Himalayas, *Inula racemosa* 'Sonnenspeer'. There are many other plants too, of course—actually a constantly changing mixture, as I experiment from one

year to the next. While it's by no means a 'natural' prairie—which couldn't exist in the woods of western New Jersey—it is an ecological one. It's a highly artificial creation, a 'novel ecosystem', a prairie of the imagination like none that ever existed in nature, but one that looks as if it belongs to its place. It's a created instrument for playing the 'music' of mood, feeling, perhaps arousing a yearning for spirituality—or for making a fright in the night.

It is an ecological garden in which every plant is adapted to the conditions of the site—but it is more than that. I wanted the garden to make physical an interior emotional world.

Methodology

How to begin the process of making a garden in a 'wild' area already filled with a population of largely unknown plants was a troubling undertaking. I certainly didn't want to kill existing growth with chemical herbicides, nor did I want to use a laborious process of smothering growth, which at a minimum could take two years. I also wanted to keep as much of the existing vegetation as possible, to keep the ground covered, and thus retain the stability of existing growth processes.

Serendipity intervened when I stumbled upon a way to start in one of Noel Kingsbury's early books, *The New Perennial Garden*, where he described planting directly into rough grass. He wrote that in certain difficult garden conditions, 'The best solution is to plant really tough, often large, perennials which will be able to compete with vigorous grasses and weeds on their own terms . . . This is the kind of planting that some garden designers call a prairie, although the plants may not all be true prairie species . . . The technique used to create such scenes is to plant in holes cut into the grass . . . The growth habit of many of these species often enables them to compete and displace grasses and weaker plants. Some are clump-formers, steadily increasing in size . . . Others are able to swamp surrounding plants with their own growth, making them particularly effective as weed suppressants.'

This was an exciting time for me. I should tell you I'm a 'book' gardener—I had no horticultural training other than the little I picked up on my own. I spent much of my time reading and learning. Even before we moved to Federal Twist, I had chanced upon a series of books about Piet Oudolf's design approach and his plant palette—*Designing with Plants* by Oudolf and Kingsbury, *Dream Plants for the Natural Garden* by Oudolf and Henk Gerritsen, and *Planting the Natural Garden* by Oudolf and Gerritsen. And, of course, I can't leave out Henk Gerritsen's *Essay on Gardening*, where I found sustenance for my fondness for weedy-looking plants, and a model for violating rules. I don't exaggerate when I say these (and a few other) books changed my life.

I had spent my entire working life as a writer in the corporate world and as I got within counting distance of retirement, I was eager for *la vita nuova*, a 'new life'. I didn't know the change would be to garden-maker, but I had my suspicions, since I had many house plants during my city life, a large collection of orchids, and a small vest-pocket Brooklyn garden for many years. In these books I first saw a Piet Oudolf garden, and the extraordinary, wildish-looking plants he was using. The photography was lush and sensuous, and I felt a deep, emotional response to the images. Some of the section titles alone—Light, Movement, Blazing, Tranquility, The Sublime, Mysticism, Life, Death—gave me a new way of conceiving what a garden could be. As Rick Darke, a prominent American writer and photographer on landscape and culture remarked to Piet in Thomas Piper's film on his work (*Five Seasons: The Gardens of Piet Oudolf*), 'You teach people things that they were unable to see.'

In these books too, especially *Designing with Plants*, I discovered concepts that were new to me—the importance of plant structure and form (spires, buttons and globes, plumes, umbels, daisies); the use of filler plants; plants used as screens and curtains; texture plants; tall emergent spikes and spires; the beauty of dying and dead plants.

I learned too about the extensive body of work on ecologies and their effects on the growth habits of perennials and grasses that German horticulturists and researchers had developed over many decades. As the only writer I knew of who was bringing this very important knowledge into English, Kingsbury remained a primary source. Through him I benefited from the work of people such as Hans Pagels and Karl Foerster and from Richard Hansen's groundbreaking book, *Perennials and their Garden Habitats in Gardens and Green Spaces (Die Stauden und Ihre Lebensbereiche in Gärten und Grünanlagen)*.

The Hansen book was a revelation. The English translation was out of print, so

I could only find a very expensive used copy. As I read it, I realized I'd already learned much of its content from Kingsbury's and Oudolf's books, but I'd never before understood the extent of ecological complexity. Hansen's studies (and Kingsbury's explication of them) revealed aspects of ecology far beyond my simple comprehension of the word—how plants live in communities, with preferences for various levels of sociability; how they have developed and utilize different mechanisms for growing and spreading, competing for light, moisture, soil, and space; and how they can be classified by preferred habitat (shade, woodland edge, open field, water's edge, and so on). It was an ecological approach to gardening, but with a depth I'd never imagined. It helped me develop a vision of gardening as something far more than decorative, but as an endeavor of complexity and meaning.

BELOW Once I had created a clearing in the woods and opened the land to the light, I began a process of experimental planting, placing plants pretty much at random, to determine which I could grow in my difficult soil.

Experiments in planting

I knew the heavy clay I was to garden on would present challenges. Most meadow environments are successful only on nutrient-poor soils. My conditions were the opposite. I would be violating all the rules. Clay is extremely rich in nutrients, and wet clay would almost certainly assure that the plants I could cultivate most successfully would grow large and fast, and be highly competitive.

Armed with that little knowledge, I began a process of experimental planting. I maintained the existing ground cover following the removal of the juniper, minimizing disturbance to the seed bank, which was waiting to burst forth into the new light. I avoided tilling or extensive digging. Richard Hansen's book, *Perennials and their Garden Habitats,* was an essential guide because it gave me an intellectual framework for understanding what I was seeing as I grew trial plants and watched their behaviors. This I learned quickly: in highly competitive conditions, only large, well-established plants are likely to survive the stress of the first few years; small plants will probably be overwhelmed. So I planted large, competitive species directly into the existing grass and weeds, using the vegetative cover to maintain stability, until the new plants could form communities and dominate the space. Eventually, I discovered that many of the species able to thrive in the conditions on the site were prairie plants native to the American Midwest, some were highly effective exotics, and others were locally native, even indigenous to the site.

I planted randomly, to get a better understanding of how conditions varied from place to place, and also to see how the appearance of various grasses and herbaceous perennials changed in different lights and atmospheric conditions. Some quite common plants, *Monarda didyma*, for example, which should have lived in wet soil, simply couldn't survive more than a year or two. I could only assume the clay wasn't to its liking or it wasn't able to live in a highly competitive environment. While I could find some large umbelliferous plants that enjoyed wet conditions, such as *Eupatorium maculatum* and *Vernonia*, other more delicate umbellifers either died off rather quickly or faded away; even Queen Anne's lace (*Daucus carota*), an attractive umbellifer and a prolific weed in our parts, couldn't grow in the wet clay.

If it had been possible, I would have adopted something like an 'Oudolfian' plant palette, but most of those plants couldn't survive in my conditions. I found a more appropriate and practical solution, using planting experiments to begin developing my own simplified selection of plants adapted to my ecology. I experimented with broadcast seeding and learned it could successfully establish new plant communities and make existing communities more complex. Random seeding of new species from outside also provided opportunity for novel combinations and unexpected, often serendipitous, effects; unwanted plants are easily removed. Even today, I continue to broadcast seed each year, adding complexity to the seed bank.

Unfortunately, nurseries in my area carried very few of the plants I had been reading about. I was still working at the time, but on weekends I would often visit a number of plant nurseries in hope of arriving when something interesting was in stock. Eventually, after making more contacts in the gardening world,

I developed a more sophisticated approach to acquiring plants—but the going was rough in the early years.

I gradually identified plants I could use with some success. One early discovery was that though some native grasses could grow in my conditions, they didn't perform well in the long term. Miscanthus, a Japanese grass, was more successful. It thrived in the clay and was able to live in highly competitive situations, I think because its basal plate and roots are very resistant to incursion from the roots and stolons of other plants. Most of the native *Panicum* species, while able to grow successfully for a time, were less resistant to incursion from other plants, and gradually succumbed to seeding in from above or infiltration from the sides, though I did find two *P. virgatum* cultivars, 'Dallas Blues' and 'Northwind', that could handle the competition rather well.

Since I was planning to make a kind of prairie, I wanted to grow prairie plants. I eventually did, but these were not easily available in those early years. I adapted by ordering seed of *Silphium perfoliatum* and *S. laciniatum* from a nursery in the Midwest and, to get *S. terebinthinaceum*, I ordered bare root plants. These were all successful, and after several years I had more of the silphiums than I needed. They are all large, have very distinctive foliage, and they flower at immense height in midsummer.

At one point, reading the plant lists of a mail order nursery in British Columbia,

Why I Hate Gardening

I hate gardening.

Rather, I hate the labor of gardening. I take great pleasure in engaging with the garden, finding new plants for the garden, thinking about future garden projects, enjoying the seasonal changes in the garden, experimenting with the garden. Other than that, my primary interest is in thinking about gardens and their meanings. I enjoy reading about gardens, visiting gardens, discussing gardens with friends, writing about gardens, but I don't care for the act of gardening and no amount of romantic writing about the pleasures of pulling weeds and digging holes can help me find pleasure in it. To be honest, I don't think I'm a great gardener. True, I'm interested in plants and how they grow, I'm a plant fanatic of a type, but my fascination is mostly with garden design, meaning, history, and the mystery and romance of the garden. This is probably the reason I first entered the realm of garden-making through reading.

About the time I started my garden, I also began writing a gardening blog called *View from Federal Twist*, in which I published essays and photographs on making my own garden, on other gardens, and on a range of subjects that interested me. After several years, I found the blog had given me a way to find community. I met other gardeners, landscape architects, garden designers, and many other people with similar interests. I began to travel to see gardens and attend conferences. People started to show interest in my garden: *The New York Times* published an article on Federal Twist, the garden appeared in several books and magazines, and was even in a Monty Don TV series called *American Gardens*. Most people who know Federal Twist know it in this way, 'at a distance', through published and electronic media. In quite a real sense, it is a garden of the imagination.

I've done a lot of imaginary gardening in my time—just not the 'real' gardening. So who does do the gardening? My gardener, Milton, comes one day a week, and has done so for 14 years. He, with his father's help in the early days, built all the stone walls, dug the ponds, moved rocks, built the gravel paths, constructed a stone circle, and planted most of the plants. And he still does most of the work to manage the garden (I, of course, provide him with a task list each week). ✯

I discovered that *Inula racemosa* 'Sonnenspeer' had been a favorite of Wolfgang Oehme—a German plantsman who was one of the founders of Oehme, van Sweden & Associates, the creators of 'New American Garden' style that transformed planting design in the US in the latter part of the 20th century. I ordered three plants, just to see what it looked like. It became a giant of the garden, one of the most characterful plants I've ever grown. Unfortunately, it seeds profusely, its one major disadvantage; however, I've learned through experience that it's a relatively short-lived plant; it quickly shoots up to maximum height and width, then grows smaller in each subsequent year. Thus, the 'logic' of its prolific seeding. It's become so important to the garden, particularly in autumn and winter, I would never consider losing it.

A vision

The word 'vision' is terribly overused, but my experience of discovering a stylistic paradigm for the garden is hard to express in any other way. Long before I started adding prairie plants to my garden trails, I was giving attention to how light fell onto my scattered plantings, so the discovery was a visual one. The position of the house and clearing in relation to the sun's path was ideal for catching the light filtering through the dark screen of trees at the back of the open clearing, and for enjoying the backlighting of grasses and perennial emergents (tall plants rising like spears from lower vegetation). The photo above shows the garden before it became a garden. This became the visual 'idea' for the design.

FRAGMENT:
Landscape of the Mind

. . . that has remained an important mental landscape for me . . .
People need things like that to go on living—mental landscapes that
have meaning for them, even if they can't explain them in words.
Haruki Murakami, *1Q84*

Sitting out in the garden, experiencing its physical presence, I often find I have drifted into a kind of alternative mental landscape, almost like sliding sideways into another dimension, perhaps while listening to the undulating sound of the cicadas, remembering a similar experience in another time, another place. Yes, memory is fundamental to making a landscape a 'place to be' in the world. I have a very good geographical memory, meaning that once I've visited a place, I usually remember it with intensity—intersections, turns, pathways, buildings, images, views—so that I carry a model of the 'landscape' in my head, and it is always tightly bound with emotion. For example, more than 20 years passed between my first and second visits to Rome, yet on that second visit, I was able to make my way about the city and, perhaps more significantly, experience powerful feelings of nostalgia when visiting the Forum, the Pantheon, the Campidoglio, and other places that had impressed themselves on my memory.

Many years later, after visiting the Forum yet again, I was strolling down the side of the Palatine Hill, doing the usual tourist things, when I saw something extraordinary—to my right a huge, prostrate Judas tree (*Cercis siliquastrum*) lying like a giant writhing snake. I was awestruck. I had been curious about this species of *Cercis* for many years, having many fond memories of its American cousin, the redbud (*Cercis canadensis*). When I was quite young, I remember walking outside with our parakeet, Budgee, on my shoulder, forgetting it might fly away, and it did just that, landing in a redbud near our house on East Academy Street. After a few moments of fear and shame for what I had done, my grandmother and I called its name until it flew down and lit on my shoulder, and I got it safely inside. There were two redbud trees planted side by side on East Academy Street, and during my early childhood I was amazed by their extraordinary habit of flowering in bunches of rich purple, directly from the dark bark, before the leaves emerged. I thought this was beautiful but it never occurred to me to say that in words.

I think I would have felt it to be inappropriate; perhaps I thought boys were not supposed to be aware of beauty. I do remember the feeling of seeing the bunched blossoms against the bark—such a sensuous juxtaposition, but for some reason mine was a mute appreciation of beauty. So my interest was already piqued when, in adulthood, I first learned of the strangely named Judas tree, *Cercis siliquastrum*, which grows in southern Europe and western Asia. To a boy from Mississippi, such exotic associations were things of wonder.

By the time I discovered the extraordinary specimen on the Palatine Hill, this had become a kind of mythic tree for me. At a much earlier time, on a much earlier visit to Rome (with landscape memories, place is important; time doesn't seem to matter), approaching St. Peter's Basilica for the first time, I remember stopping to examine a bronze panel of the Holy Door showing the Crucifixion. The following words were on the panel beneath the crucified Christ and two thieves: *Hodie mecum eris in paradiso* (Today you will be with me in paradise). Though I am not religious, I understood the meaning of the words, and was tremendously moved. My long-discarded upbringing in the Southern Baptist Church may have had some role in this—I had heard the power of the words 'Today thou shalt be with me in paradise' many times in my early life. But there were other sources of powerful emotional response buried in memory. Far more important for me was the Latin word for 'today'—*hodie*—a joyful sound filled with music and celebration ever since I first heard it when a friend in college introduced me to Benjamin Britten's *A Ceremony of Carols*.

This wonderfully random conglomeration of places, objects, images, memories, sounds, and words had created a powerful inner 'landscape' that remains—probably only one of a multitude of potential landscapes of memory and emotion that lie latent, waiting for some stimulus to awaken them. In that timeless moment, place, meaning, and feelings are one.

DESIGNING AN AMERICAN LANDSCAPE GARDEN

Kent's genius lay in the way he used simple
features . . . to create strong atmospheres
and a state of perpetual curiosity in the visitor.
There is no set itinerary round the garden,
and each garden episode has more than one
entrance or exit point, so it feels as if there
is always more to explore . . . The pulsating
strangeness of the place . . . lends it a
mysterious, disjointed tone that makes for
a genuinely transcendent visiting experience.

Tim Richardson, on Rousham, in *The Arcadian
Friends: Inventing the English Landscape Garden*

Federal Twist is a landscape garden, not a traditional garden. It has no lawns, no flower beds, as such, only a naturally shaped landscape, a surface layered by perennials, grasses, shrubs, and a few understory trees. You move about on a series of paths that, all told, are far longer than you might expect in a relatively small garden. You are immersed in vegetation. Along the way are stone walls, reflecting pools, several small areas for lingering, and a small pond teeming with dragonflies, frogs, and other aquatic life. The purpose of the garden is reflection and pleasure— the simple pleasure of sitting out on the terrace overlooking the garden, feeling the inconstant breeze, listening to sycamore (*Platanus occidentalis*) leaves rustling above, to birdsong in the forest and to frogs croaking and splashing in the water below; exploring the pathways, many hidden by the abundant growth of midsummer, catching the light and shadow as they cross the land, glimpsing moments of intimacy—and for experiencing the marvels of memory, nostalgia, and feeling. The garden has no utilitarian purpose whatsoever, unless you allow for a human utility, a place to experience the atmosphere and the mood of the day, to think, to talk, to muse, to remember, to be.

Why do I call Federal Twist a landscape garden, not just a naturalistic garden? It violates many expectations of a landscape garden, certainly those of the 18th-century English landscape garden with its broad sweep of Picturesque landforms, water, forest, sky, classical follies and ruins so prominent in the paintings of artists, such as Claude Lorraine, who were the impetus for that style. I twist the concept a bit—quite a bit. One main reason is evident if you look at the image (next page) of the sun rising behind the wall of trees on the far side of the garden, opposite the house, or the second image (pages 70-1) showing the long view of the garden with immense trees in the distance. These images make it dramatically clear that important elements of the garden are 'capabilities' of the landscape, not part of the garden at all. I didn't make them; I simply recognized them and their value.

Back at the beginning, when I started the garden, I already recognized the landscape had a characterful identity and atmosphere. Any garden I might make would have to work with that landscape. Making the landscape part of the garden and the garden part of the landscape was my aim from the start. I wanted to anchor the garden in the landscape so there would be no visible boundary between one and the other. I wanted the garden and landscape to feel they were one. To do this required exaggerating views, manipulating scale, using simple, appropriate materials such as the local stone, amplifying it a bit by making it into walls and simple structures, adding an abundance of paths, using plants with a wildish quality, keeping dead tree snags—all toward the end of making the landscape garden appear effortless and at ease with itself.

Balancing the idea of the visual 'landscape garden' was my decision to make Federal Twist park-like. It is a garden of paths, and has as its primary purpose walking and exploring the landscape. Though you can stop and see the details, the focus is on the idea of landscape—the clearing in the woods, an American landscape, but one that faintly recalls its precedents in another time, across an ocean.

If it were possible, I'd have the garden open for anyone to visit at any time, just as you might a public park.

Although Federal Twist is in a historical lineage that descends from other garden traditions, it makes no pretense to be what it isn't. It is a distinctively American landscape type—a clearing in the woods—rather common here because of our extensive woodlands and history of living in them. America does not have the centuries of cultural history found in Europe and many other parts of the world—nothing like the layers of history you find in the UK, for example, where structures and artefacts perhaps several thousand years old may be uncovered in a field of cabbages. In contrast, Federal Twist feels rather recent,

ABOVE The sun rising through the trees on the far side of the garden illustrates the importance of the surrounding landscape. At sunrise, much of the garden is unseen in the shadows below.

THE VIEW FROM FEDERAL TWIST

even transient—as if it might just disappear, be absorbed back into the woods.

It is an American landscape garden, but I do not mean it is representative of American gardens; it has no lawn, it is 'untidy', it is rough, and its boundaries are not obvious at all because they blend with the surrounding woods. It is the antithesis of most gardens and yards of suburbia where utility reigns, where foundation plantings closely hug houses and the use of trees and perennial plantings is stinted so they will not be impediments to mowing, where there is little room left for imagination, inspiration, contemplation.

Its design also is influenced by the idea of wilderness, of the forest and forest life, of the vast Midwestern prairies and meadow-like settings in the East, and by the strivings of some aspects of the American psyche, such as the vague desire to escape urban life for the country. Federal Twist resonates with the voices of such early American idealists as Henry David Thoreau and Ralph Waldo Emerson, leaders of the Transcendentalist movement in the period of early intellectual awakening on this continent, in a time when forest was a far more pervasive landscape than today. In *Nature*, Emerson wrote:

> In the woods, we return to reason and faith . . . Standing on the bare
> ground,—my head bathed by the blithe air, and uplifted into infinite
> space,—all mean egotism vanishes. I become a transparent eye-ball;
> I am nothing; I see all; the currents of the Universal Being circulate
> through me; I am part or particle of God.

These words are classic in the American literary canon (and surprisingly reflect both German Romanticism and Asian religious precepts), but from the perspective of today, they sound distant and faint, even quaint.

Can a garden still be redemptive, transformative? Can it bring place and meaning together? It is very difficult even to raise those questions in the American culture of today.

Starting out

As I thought about what the garden would become, the informal style of the house, its woodland location, and its odd siting at an acute angle to the property boundary (to orient the house toward the sun in winter)—all suggested an intimate, modest, asymmetrical design approach . . . a kind of bowing to the spirit of the place. I had no doubt the garden would be naturalistic, and it would merge seamlessly with the surrounding green woods.

Moving from concept to design

After cutting trees, clearing the garden space, mowing to reveal the land surface, I had to move from concept—a clearing in the woods—to a more precise design plan. I thought about how the garden could retain something of the original spirit of place I first encountered here. During the experimental planting, I paid close

RIGHT Rounding a path from the woodland garden to the open 'landscape garden', the changes in scale, the light, the sky make the garden, though relatively small, seem immense. This is of course an illusion but, for the briefest moment, you may think you're in another century, another place.

attention to the ecology of the site, variations in habitat, appropriate planting, and, on a more abstract level, the mood and atmosphere of the place. I was concerned with how to slowly and gently coax the ungardened landscape into becoming a garden. Visualizing the process as layering the garden, one bit at a time, into the existing landscape and ecology, I wanted to fit the pieces in as they came to me—meaning to fit in ideas as well as plants.

But apart from the desire to preserve the mood of the place, I was hesitant to move forward with a clear design decision. I was reluctant to take action. I was stalled thinking about concepts, not about the physical garden; I was avoiding making a decision, and needed a push. (I'd later learn anything can be undone and redone, and I now accept even disasters with equanimity.)

Something pushed. Did I? Or was it an accident?

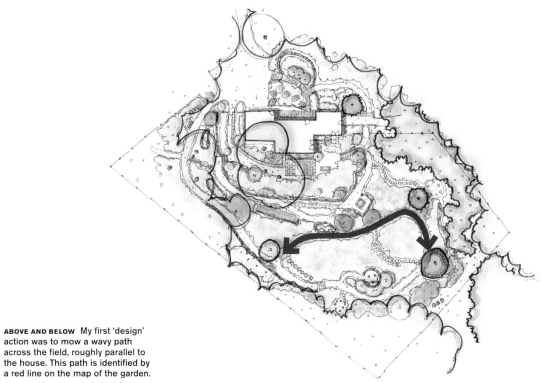

ABOVE AND BELOW My first 'design' action was to mow a wavy path across the field, roughly parallel to the house. This path is identified by a red line on the map of the garden.

A topographic surprise

I expected to learn a bit and make slow progress in deciding on a design plan, but a simple action I took changed everything. The next step was like an epiphany. I knew I needed to better understand the topography of the land, how water would flow across it, what plants were naturally growing where, to determine how to place plants to make best use of the site ecology. As a kind of rough topographic survey, and almost in exasperation, I mowed a single wavy path across the center of the garden space, roughly parallel to the house. This simple action started the design.

A stroke of artifice can make meaning. Wallace Stevens expressed this idea with humor and precision in this well-known poem.

Anecdote of the Jar

I placed a jar in Tennessee,
And round it was, upon a hill.
It made the slovenly wilderness
Surround that hill.

The wilderness rose up to it,
And sprawled around, no longer wild.
The jar was round upon the ground
And tall and of a port in air.

It took dominion everywhere.
The jar was gray and bare.
It did not give of bird or bush,
Like nothing else in Tennessee.

Making that rough path was like placing that strange jar in Tennessee—in a crazy, unexpected place. My garden would be different from any gardens I knew. It would be strange and new and would 'not give of bird or bush, like nothing else in Tennessee'—not for the sake of strangeness, but for the sake of the place.

Where before I was not able to make sense of the space, that path revealed subtle variations in topography, wetter and dryer spots, and locations of existing plant communities. I had direct access to cut-away views of plants I couldn't even see before. It gave me an almost infinite series of reference points. For the first time, I was able to 'know' the land almost as if it had a body and personality. That rough path helped me understand the ecology of the land in a way that I could not understand it before, and the garden sprang to life, at least in my mind.

At that point, I made my first intentional planting. Without any soil preparation, since I didn't want to disturb the seed bank, I planted a 60ft (18m) drift of large *Filipendula rubra* 'Venusta' on the far side of the path, directly into the existing vegetation, in an area I knew to be a damper part of the garden. I used large, well-established plants, having learned from my experiments that I had to work with plants of substantial size that could quickly establish, cover the ground, and shade out weeds if they were to thrive in the competitive environment. Mass is important in my garden—both by addition and subtraction—in several ways and at different times of year.

THE VIEW FROM FEDERAL TWIST

LEFT Minimizing disturbance of the soil surface, I planted a long sweep of *Filipendula rubra* 'Venusta' along one side of that central path. Apart from mowing, I did not make any attempt to remove existing vegetation.

Making that first path, and the financial investment in so many large plants, I realized I had already begun designing. So I continued to read the land, and let it guide me.

The story I'm telling clearly shows my design approach is intuitive. I did take measurements and draw a few crude plans early in making the garden, but those were to help me understand the space of the garden, to determine how far back to push the wall of trees across from the house, and to make other basic decisions, certainly nothing like detailed design plans. Details of the design happened as I worked on the ground, in the developing garden, responding to what I saw in the moment.

Hydrology becomes design

During heavy rain, a tremendous amount of stormwater flows from the high point of the ridge above the Delaware, across Federal Twist Road, around the south end of the house, then out into the main garden below the house, which

OPPOSITE A tremendous volume of water flows across the land surface during heavy rains. The map shows how this pattern of water flow became a kind of design template, suggesting the overall layout of the garden, which resembles a miniature river delta.

BELOW The Lockatong Creek.

THE VIEW FROM FEDERAL TWIST

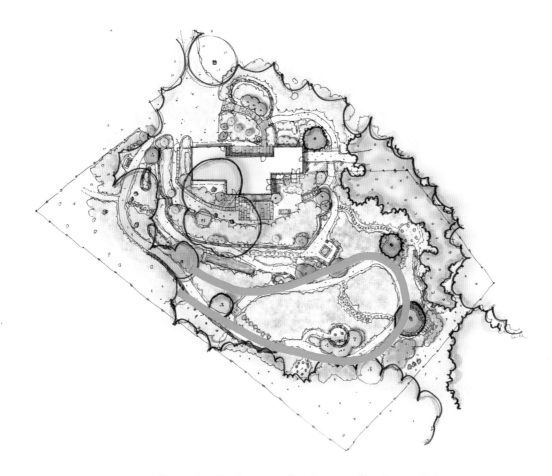

itself lies on a slope that falls gradually down to Lockatong Creek, a pristine stream far below. That gentle slope was both a significant design constraint and an opportunity. I later learned—another step in reading the landscape—that the water flow over the ground, the hydrology of the land, would be a template. The design of the garden, its paths, the placement of plant communities and structural elements, would all be influenced by the hydrology of the site and its effect on soil moisture.

In plan view, the shape of the garden would take the form of an elongated, curved teardrop following the water flow around the house, then sweeping outward like a small river delta. Plants that could thrive in wet conditions were a natural choice and, since many of these plants are very large and mature late, the garden would become an immersive experience in summer and autumn.

Adding complexity

As I lived with the garden through several seasons and observed its cyclical changes, visited many other gardens, read widely in the literature of garden design and landscape architecture, and perhaps most importantly met other garden-makers, I came to realize how much more the garden could be.

I continued to add layers through new plantings, seeding, and creating new, though minimal, structure over the years, making the garden more complex. I wanted to celebrate the emotive power of light and shade, of sound, movement, fragrance, and other intangible aspects of the garden. I understood that the garden could awaken memories, relate to the past life of the place, and evoke mystery, the numinous and ineffable. And I came to know a perceptible 'spirit of place', a felt presence.

This occurs unexpectedly, in certain moments, when the garden evokes strong feelings—often in autumn and early winter, in early morning or twilight, when it takes on a strange beauty, with luminous colors followed by browns and tans and grays, the disintegrating, remnant structures of plants creating striking abstract

LEFT Weather and lighting conditions can evoke scenes of strong emotion, most often in early morning or at twilight. Here an almost explosive swirl of damp grasses seems to glow in the wetness of a rainy, foggy morning.

BELOW The damp leaning spires of *Inula racemosa* 'Sonnenspeer' and a miscanthus create a melancholy scene of repose.

displays. We naturally turn to meaning when reminded of the ends of things, when we observe shimmering specters of death in the garden.

Legibility

I imagined a wild garden full of complexity, a simulacrum of a wet prairie almost bordering on chaos—complex but legible, able to be easily read as an intentionally aesthetic creation. Much of our expectation of landscapes and gardens comes to us from other cultures and gardening traditions of the past. In many cases, we still hold those ideas in some form. In *Planting in a Post-Wild World*, Thomas Rainer

and Claudia West explain some of the reasons for differing concepts of 'naturalness': 'Much of the Western world has inherited a concept of naturalness that is tied to an 18th-century British concept of the picturesque. Our preference for long views, open landscapes, clean edges, and just a touch of mystery has influenced all aspects of our built landscapes. As a result, the general public has very little tolerance for wild, illegible landscapes and plantings.' Other garden traditions too have influenced a preference for more formal structure in gardens, one prominent example being the Arts and Crafts garden of rooms, as well as other gardens that rely largely on hedges, topiary, or hardscape for structure. While naturalistic gardens have become far more widely accepted over the past several decades, many people still remain resistant to naturalism in gardens and struggle to see order in the underlying ecology that is revealed in plant growth patterns and structure.

Because of this predisposition for certain other landscape types, legibility is essential in naturalistic planting. When a planting has great diversity, especially when it confounds traditional expectations, as in my interpretation of a prairie, the planting must be coherent and immediately understandable. One way to accomplish this is by creating a perception of order through repetition of shape, form, texture, and color. To some extent, this can be accomplished on the ground

plain (the plan view). But this is effective only when vegetation is low and patterning and textures are especially strong. When plants mature, however, perception of order is enhanced by using tall structural plants and massed plantings with highly distinctive shapes (like silhouettes) and distinctive textures and colors. As the eye sweeps across the garden, similarities in size, shape, massing, texture, and color make the plants and plant groupings easily legible and show design intent.

Although I've called the planting at peak growth almost chaotic, I exaggerate; it isn't chaotic by any means, though the plantings can be extremely complex. Some look like abstract art, but it is even more essential that abstract compositions be legible—that the forms of individual plants retain their distinctive shapes and characters, that colors and textures contribute aesthetically, that individual elements of the planting work visually to give a sense of the ecological order underlying the garden. Often the visual effects of some plantings suggest abstract paintings in particular and, though I don't mean to suggest that gardens should 'imitate' paintings in any way, the visual and emotional effects can be strikingly similar. I've frequently recognized similarities between photographs of my garden in late stages of dissolution and some expressionist paintings of ravaged landscapes by Anselm Kiefer.

Legibility can occur in simple and complex ways. The images on this page show primarily vertical plant forms against dark backgrounds. The plants are easily legible as the eye passes across a range of vertical structures, colors and individual shapes. On the opposite page, the diverse mixture of plants, some tilting diagonally, and the partially hidden sculpture make a much more complex picture. The eye takes a second or two to make sense of the space and the objects distributed within it.

TOP Verticals of *Inula racemosa* 'Sonnenspeer', *Silphium perfoliatum*, a leaning *Silphium laciniatum*, the faded bronze clouds of *Filipendula rubra* flower heads all create a fizz of energy against the background.

CENTER LEFT TO RIGHT A spire of *Silphium laciniatum* towers over filipendula flowering in pink. Inula and *Silphium perfoliatum* rise above miscanthus foliage. White linear flowers of *Sanguisorba canadensis* amazingly (because their structure is so fragile) remain vertical in twilight.

BOTTOM The empty space between two loose plant groupings of *Silphium perfoliatum*, *Dipsacus fullonum*, a tall, slim *Silphium terebinthinaceum* flower stalk, and a variety of other tall or to-be-tall plants subtly defines a pathway through them.

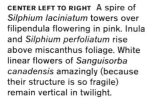

So legibility can occur in both relatively simple and complex ways; it isn't just about being able to recognize repetitive structure in a group of plants. Legibility also encompasses a sophisticated ability to recognize order in complexity. Even an abstract painting can train the eye in ways to see and interpret aspects of the naturalistic garden. The Keifer reference above is a case in point. I saw his painting, *The Order of the Angels*, a giant canvas, at the Art Institute of Chicago many years ago, before I made my garden. The extremely powerful work appears to portray a field of destruction; to my eye it's clearly a landscape. Seeing this painting planted visual ideas I would later find in my own garden. In this case, the 'idea' of legibility preceded even the existence of my garden.

Another element to improve legibility is limiting the numbers of distinct species. In other words, simplicity improves legibility. Since my soil constrains the range of plants I can grow, the available selection of plant shapes in the garden is less varied than in many gardens, reducing the probability of too much visual diversity and, by default, enhancing legibility.

Lessons in legibility

TOP RIGHT AND FAR RIGHT: *Carex crinita* mixed with *Lobelia siphilitica* (right) and *Iris pseudacorus* (far right) both splay out to the left, and thus have superficially similar forms, but their characters and effects are very different. The carex and lobelia leap out toward light and space, suggesting a yearning for more as the plants grow rapidly in early summer. The autumnal iris leaves, broken, falling, yellowing, though strongly evocative, make a dramatic dying gesture.

BOTTOM RIGHT AND FAR RIGHT
The large, highly dissected leaves of *Silphium laciniatum* (right), though the same orange-brown color as the background, are easily legible to anyone who knows this highly distinctive plant. Leaves of the same plant (far right), still green and brightly backlit against a dark background, are even more easily legible.

CENTER LEFT Prairie view in early autumn, with shafts of sunlight creating a chiaroscuro effect. To an eye used to seeing meadow-like plantings, this is easily legible but perhaps less so for a viewer familiar with more traditional gardens. The well-lit woodland background points up the importance of context, so the prairie becomes visible as a thickly planted mass of herbaceous perennials and grasses. In particular, the plumes of miscanthus flowering in the left back, the fading pinkish plumes of filipendula, and the reflections off leaf surfaces help define the prairie, though the overall effect is certainly impressionistic.

CENTER MIDDLE Blackish seed pods on a branch of *Baptisia alba*, present a strongly evocative image, even for a viewer not familiar with this plant. Though the background is busy, even rather decorative, the subject is easily legible.

CENTER RIGHT Another prairie view in summer. Again, the dark background at the top of the photo provides context, making it clear the main subject is a prairie thick with plants. The tall perennials flowering against the dark background, the differentiation of shapes by color, and the different orientations of plant stems and flower heads make the prairie, though impressionistic, still easily legible.

Structure to indicate intentionality: paniculate hydrangea flower heads against the light of the setting sun (top); miscanthus shapes against the woodland edge (middle); sunlit miscanthus (bottom). All are scenic views of plant shapes, amplified by light.

Early on I could see the need for more structure to contain the feeling of wildness and to indicate intentionality. Among Americans in particular, with their national fixation on the neat, suburban front lawn, this 'fear of the wild'—or perhaps I should say fear of the social opprobrium of not having a neat, well-cared-for lawn—can be an obstacle to acceptance of 'looser' styles. I have had visitors who had no interest in walking in the garden, and some who showed obvious discomfort, even fear, or on venturing into the garden wanted quickly to return to the safe environment of the terrace.

Use of 'orderly frames' is one method to make such gardens more visually accessible to people unfamiliar with the look of natural landscapes. I had been practicing a variation of this 'framing' concept by using paths, stone walls, and other features to make visible orderly processes at work, and I felt a pleasurable surprise when I first encountered the term 'orderly frames' in Rainer's and West's book. They attribute the origin of the concept and name to Joan Iverson Nassauer. Nassauer uses the term broadly and has suggested this idea as one of several

LEFT The hard structure of pathways and the space above them gives plants breathing room, making them more legible.

'cues to care' to address the inability of many to 'see' the order in ecological and naturalistic plantings. With that same goal, I used the stone on the property to make walls and other structures that serve as framing devices. I also found that other structural elements, in this case focal points—reflecting pools, a large stone circle, minimalist sculpture, structural benches and chairs—work well to create 'centers of attraction' (alternative 'framing devices') around which the rambunctious plantings could visually coalesce, fixed points that draw the eye and visually anchor the garden into the landscape (much as that jar in Tennessee).

A word on 'built' or 'made' structure, which is simply my opinion. In a naturalistic garden, structure needs to be composed of simple, natural materials, preferably from the site or the area, and be appropriate to the place. Elaborate structures can easily destroy a subtle sense of place and spoil the effect of the garden. If present, a more complex structure (such as a swimming pool or pool house) should be isolated, shielded from view, and well designed so its use does not affect the garden itself. Nor is the naturalistic landscape garden an art gallery. I know I'm going against some well-established tradition in this respect, but I feel strongly that a garden made for the display of sculpture is simply a landscaped art gallery, not a garden (always allowing for exceptions to rules). Any sculptural element used in a naturalistic garden should be subtle, minimalist, and low impact, not calling attention to itself in a way that draws attention from the garden and its processes, causes confusion, or conflicts with the spirit of place; it should contribute to the atmosphere and meaning of the garden.

I have three pieces of minimalist sculpture in the garden. Two are cast bronze sculptures created by a friend, Marc Rosenquist. Both of these are abstract shapes that blend easily with the shapes and colors of plants. They resemble seed pods or abstract plant parts and almost vanish when the garden is in full growth. But in winter and spring, their simple shapes give the eye a place to pause, and their hard surfaces and permanent presence help the garden to speak, even when it is virtually empty of plants. A third is a red Alexander Calderesque mobile, hanging from a large tree at a focal point at the back of the garden. More a bauble than art, its good-humored red circles complement the green of the forest in warmer seasons and in winter it offers movement and a spot of color on dreary days.

Although manmade 'frames' visually contain the garden, they are conceptual frames, not boundaries. The stone walls amplify the linearity and curvature of pathways, more clearly defining structure, but they are simply outlines; when a path curves, the accompanying wall curves. One wiggly wall stands alone, but it also separates a more cultivated part of the garden from an 'outside' area leading into the darker woods; it acts as a marker and a focal point. A large stone circle serves as a kind of visual 'heart' of the garden. The wiggly wall, circle, and reflecting pools are all focal points, framing devices of a different kind. When the garden is at full growth, many of the framing devices become much less visible among the immersive growth, and then the pathways take on that role, helping you experience structure and discriminate between garden and 'other'. They enable you to see the garden as both a structured entity and a unity, almost as a living organism. If you look at the garden from above, you easily see the analogy to a giant living cell.

LEFT Use of 'orderly frames' is an important technique for making naturalistic landscapes visually accessible to people unfamiliar with their look. Above, the hard form of a bronze sculpture gives the eye a place to rest while the mind makes sense of the surrounding loose planting. Center, the square pool and gravel surround clearly define a scene that visually organizes the loose planting around it. Bottom, the reflection in the pool shows yet another kind of legibility, 'framing' the reflected view like a work of art.

RIGHT Though they certainly do not literally 'frame' the wild-looking vegetation, these two intricately structured chairs, designed and produced by Dan Benarcik, a well-known garden designer at Chanticleer, near Philadelphia, perform a similar framing function by, in effect, bringing order to chaos (consider T. S. Eliot's 'At the still point of the turning world').

BELOW Obscured in shadowy twilight, the dark, moody pathway curving around the bank and up to the terrace, which is totally hidden here, creates a framework for understanding this place and how to move through it.

Over time, the stone walls have taken on an additional aesthetic and atmospheric function—the visual swerve of a long arc of stone outlining a curving gravel path guides the eye deeper into the garden, while the stone circle, though rarely used for any practical purpose, suggests mystery, hinting at some unknown ceremony or rite. So too, a circle of upright log seats in an adjacent area suggests some kind of undefined, perhaps mysterious, gathering place. They also simply make a good place to sit and take in the view across the garden to the house or to watch the light of the setting sun glimmer through the trees up in the woodland garden.

ABOVE The curving stone wall and gravel path, accented by three miscanthus in contrasting colors, create a strong frame for the edge of the garden as it meets the surrounding ungardened forest.

Hedges

I made minimal use of hedges as frames and formal structures to indicate intentionality amid the profuse plantings. I had not originally intended to use hedging at all. I did greatly admire the contrasting hedges in Piet Oudolf's early

version of Hummelo, though I couldn't contemplate anything as ambitious as Piet's geometrical hedges (and they eventually died from wet soil).

In the early years, when the planting was still rather loose and spotty, I felt I needed to introduce some formality to visually stabilize the billowy masses of grasses and perennials. What I settled on happened to be another unexpected act, almost an impulse reminiscent of the first path I cut across the bare garden space in 2005. I made a straight hedge at the south end of the garden, using several *Thuja occidentalis* 'Smaragd'. I chose thuja, which is commonly called arborvitae in the US and is overused in suburbia (it's become a joke among designers), because it grows well in wet conditions. I'd also recently seen mature *Thuja occidentalis* on Mount Desert Island in Maine and, for the first time, realized it grows into a beautiful and imposing large forest tree. I didn't want mine to grow that large, but simply seeing the mature tree in its natural setting 'rescued' it, in my mind, from its suburban oblivion.

LEFT I also used hedges as 'orderly frames' to temper the wild look of the garden. Here, a line of *Thuja occidentalis* 'Smaragd' separates an outer pathway from the larger garden and provides a dark, evergreen contrast to the changeable masses of herbaceous perennials and grasses. This hedge is also a wall that provides visual relief and a bit of quietness as you pass behind it.

BELOW At a far end of the garden, I wanted a formal stop, like a fermata in music, where the garden ends and rougher woods begin. I also needed to hide an 8-ft (2.5-m) deer exclusion fence. So I planted an L-shaped hedge of European hornbeam (*Carpinus betulus*) and made a shady sitting area hidden by several paniculate hydrangeas. This is the only really formal element in the garden.

This is a hedge but I think of it more as a wall. From the path on the far side, the view of the garden is blocked entirely. This gives me, and I hope you too, a moment of calm and relief. For a moment, you enter a space entirely different from other parts of the garden.

At a far edge of the garden, where I had placed a wooden bench behind a group of hydrangeas, I needed a screen to obscure the deer fence immediately behind the bench and to create the perception of a sharp end to the garden. In this case, I wanted an even more formal hedge. I decided to use European hornbeam (*Carpinus betulus*), planted to make an L-shaped screen. Though I would have preferred to buy mature plants, they would have cost far more than I could afford, so I ordered them bare-root from a mail-order nursery in Oregon. They took about ten years to reach hedge size, but they now give that corner a comforting feeling of refuge.

I have to admit this planned 'end' to the garden has become rather permeable over the years. I occasionally put extra plants I have no immediate use for into

this holding area beyond the hedge, and so I'm slowly extending the garden further into the ungardened edge.

A third hedge isn't really a hedge so much as an irregular line of boxwood extending from the end of a long, narrow pond (which I call the 'canal pond') into the middle of the garden. I love the smell of boxwood in the summer—memories from my childhood in Mississippi—and I always admired the irregularly pruned box in Jacques Wirtz's home garden in Antwerp, Belgium, though mine unfortunately look nothing like his. The original intent was to have

the line of box visually extend the line of the pond further into the garden, thus carrying the eye more deeply into the center. That concept never worked as intended (it wasn't easily legible). So I interrupted the intended line, took the space between the box and the pond, and planted a large mass of petasites there. Fed by the wetness of the pond, the petasites now grows into a gunnera-like mass that links the pond and the box hedge. The original concept of a long linear feature is lost, but I'm more pleased with the replacement petasites 'bouquet', which is almost baroque in appearance.

Paths

At the very beginning of the design process in 2006 I was fixated on paths and how they would relate to the plantings. Over many years, I did a little of both planting and path-making simultaneously, adding small paths as it became obvious to me where they were needed, but it was essential to lay out the major pathways early on. I first made an elongated oval pathway very roughly outlining the imaginary river delta as it swept around the house and away down the slope. This path more or less followed the border of the garden. After I decided that the first path across the center of the garden would be a permanent part of the design, this oval path was the major feature, and the physical reference for positioning almost everything else.

I used wood chips left from the tree-cutting to make the first paths, but that was never satisfactory. The wood chips washed away in heavy rain, so I needed something heavier and more permanent. I had no hesitation about material. I wanted gravel, a small size we call 'Delaware pea gravel', for the feel and the sound of walking on it, and because it is practical and durable. Making the main gravel paths was a three-year project, and my method was a seat-of-the-pants approach to design and construction. I never considered going to an outside contractor—that would have been far more efficient, but also very disruptive and

BELOW I took advantage of a slight rise in elevation to introduce a gentle curve as this path passes the canal pond (invisible to its left) and around to the woodland garden and the terrace hidden above. The late western sun sends shards of golden light into the shade.

LEFT AND BELOW Multiple paths, some large, some small, weave throughout the garden.

ABOVE In this drone view, two main paths emerge from the woodland garden in the upper right to become a more complex network of curves weaving throughout the main garden. The large planting in the center is the prairie, which has no pathways. Access isn't possible simply because the growth is too thick. (And because I feel a part of the garden should remain inaccessible.)

expensive. I wanted to move slowly, to give myself time to think, to try and fail, to change my mind.

Periodically I would have a truckload of gravel delivered to the driveway in front of the house, and Milton and his father would take it from there. Using only shovels and a sturdy hand cart, they would move it several hundred feet to the back of the house, gradually building up the paths. The process was the traditional one—to lay a geotextile fabric, which helped prevent the gravel sinking into the wet clay, and served to some extent as a weed barrier, then a layer of larger chipped gravel, then a finish layer of Delaware pea gravel.

The finished paths are 6–8in (15–20cm) above the adjacent grade and make a comfortable walking surface, even in rain. They have served well for many years, but gravel is a wonderful medium for seeding in, so they must be cleaned well at least once a year. Milton rakes out seedlings in early summer and I occasionally do a path clean-up using a hand-held propane torch.

I like to meander in a garden, so deciding where paths would go was an intermittent process carried out over several years as I discovered where more paths might add to the sense of exploration and discovery. I was also influenced by Noel Kingsbury's description of the networks of large and single-person pathways in the Westpark in Munich. Though I did not begin with the intent of using the Westpark concept as a model, it stayed in my mind and certainly influenced me in the decision to continue making paths, both wide and narrow, beyond those I originally anticipated. I find it rather amazing I was so influenced by path layout in a park in Germany that I had never even seen—simply by an idea.

The main oval pathway was a distance from the house, starting about midway out and curving around through the back of the property. I connected that oval pathway to the outside world by adding long paths that extended past each end of the house to the front, where parking and the entry garden are, and where plants and materials would be delivered.

ABOVE A path, passing through a simple planting of amsonia, miscanthus, and ligularia, illustrates the importance of the empty space above pathways. The space identifies passage for movement, even when the paths themselves may be hidden by tall vegetation, and it suggests the importance of paths as breathing spaces for the garden.

In a second phase of path-making, I added paths much nearer the house to provide easy access via stairs to the terrace overlooking the garden, and several smaller linkages to encourage exploration of formerly inaccessible areas—places where you can linger, rest, and feel alone with the garden. Later I added more smaller paths at the fringes of the garden to further encourage exploration and to provide access to out-of-the-way places.

The garden pushes back

When I came to think about movement through the garden, I wanted to make it slow and indirect. Though the garden is not large, I intended it to have a spatial fluidity that invites you to wander and take a different way through each time. In this sense it's highly permeable, though it doesn't appear so at certain times of year, such as late summer, when many paths are hidden by the immersive mass of the garden. There are also parts of the garden you can't enter simply because the plants take up all the available space. The garden, in a sense, 'pushes back' a bit, offers just a little resistance.

Visitors often ask me to tell them which way to go to see the garden. This isn't a question I can answer. I've visited many gardens, and I can't think of a single one that has a 'start here' sign. You simply plunge in and find your way. There is no single way to go around Federal Twist and see it in one pass. You have to select a path and start walking, and as you come to another path, you decide which way looks most interesting to you. Even better—you just wander. I designed the

BELOW Parts of the garden are impassible, intentionally, because certain areas are thickly planted and there are no paths through. When a visitor wants to find a way to move to a specific place, the way to get there may not be clear. The garden may seem to push back a bit.

garden to encourage exploration and attention to detail—to put you in a relationship with the garden.

Because the plantings are massive and tall, at times you can see only the path in front of you; the only way out is forward—to follow a path without knowing its destination. In this way, you encounter the garden. Only by allowing the garden to reveal itself, perhaps to challenge what you think a garden should be, will you find the experience interesting, useful or rewarding, and perhaps enjoyable. You have to give yourself up to it, to give the garden agency, to recognize you are part of the process of the garden. If you hear hints of 'deep ecology' in this, it is probably so.

My first conscious experience with this 'push back' happened when I discovered that some visitors couldn't easily make their own way through. They would approach me as if lost, and this appeared to be an unusual experience for them. Since the garden is only slightly over 1½ acres (0.6 ha) in size, at first I thought these were simply people who might get lost any place, but it happened frequently enough that I had to accept the evidence of others. Most 'lost' visitors did not find the disorientating experience unpleasant; in fact, they often remarked on how much they enjoyed the garden, how different it was from most other gardens they had seen.

So as I began to explore my own motivations for making numerous pathways through often very tall vegetation, I realized my intent had been to make a garden I could, in a sense, get lost in. The experience is like giving over control, being

ABOVE When the passage ahead seems impenetrable, it's probably best to stop, relax, take a look around and then, if the way isn't obvious, just plunge ahead. The goal is to encourage visitors to encounter the garden, to be in relationship to the garden in some way, to become aware of the spirit of the place.

open to feeling the garden push back a bit, and allowing the garden to take charge.

My first experience with this 'push back' in another garden occurred several years later, on my first visit to Broughton Grange in Oxfordshire. Broughton Grange was designed by Tom Stuart-Smith, perhaps one of the more 'intellectual' garden designers in the UK. I had long admired the garden in photographs, particularly what appeared to be a grand centerpiece, a large, rectangular pool of water in the middle of the garden with a row of beautiful stepping stones across one side leading the eye off into the landscape. I had imagined a day when I could walk in that space, along the water, and across the stepping stones. It was an extremely enticing prospect. As imagined, it would be an easy, idyllic experience; nature (and the garden) would benignly accede to my wishes.

All this was a fantasy that bore little relation to the truth of the garden I found there. The square of water was so large, and so placed, that it blocked easy circulation through a large part of the garden. It felt like an obstacle, though a beautiful one. And with broad plantings, changes in level, limited pathways around the pool, and pathways that ended at the pool edge, it was a bit challenging to navigate, to get where I thought I wanted to be. This was my first notice that things were not as I had imagined. I felt a little surprised but I explored and

BELOW My first experience with 'push back' from another garden occurred several years after I felt it in my own garden. It happened at Broughton Grange in Oxfordshire in a garden designed by Tom Stuart-Smith.

found my way through, even discovered some delights, such as a dark tunnel of hedges with a distant view out a cut-away 'window' at the end. As I explored my way to the pool's edge, I was enjoying the garden from many different points of view, and the views out were stunningly beautiful.

And then the 'stepping stones', which I had imagined walking across so many times in years past; they were in fact very large, and so spaced, that they did not make for an easy walk across the water (certainly not for me); they were more an impediment to walking. As I crossed them, I felt the passage was a little precarious. I could stand on one stone and feel as if it were a little island, but stepping across the intervening water from stone to stone required very close attention. I felt the stones were intended more as unique places for observation (perhaps more to be thought about than walked on) and not an easy path across the water.

I was forced to slow down, to stop, in fact, and rethink how to approach 'seeing' this remarkable garden. To paraphrase Tom Stuart-Smith, I had discovered, in a physical way, that the garden was not about me, that I was not in charge—the garden was. I recall I quickly left the stepping stones after crossing the water once, and took a comfortable seat on the opposite side where I could relax, enjoy the view across the garden into the valley beyond, and think about what had just happened.

I encountered this concept again the following year, but in a very different way, when I discovered a talk on the internet that Tom had given at the Garden Museum Literary Festival. That talk was especially intriguing because it seemed to confirm what I had experienced on my visit. Speaking about Broughton Grange, he said, 'When you cross over the threshold into a garden . . . you see things in a different way and, particularly, you see that you as an individual are not the center of what's going on . . . One of the most important things for me is that the middle of the garden is left empty. Because if the middle of the garden is empty, you can't be there. It's about the garden, and the processes of nature. The process of the garden takes primacy in the place.'

I believe what I experienced in my garden as 'push back' is similar to what Tom means when he said 'The process of the garden takes primacy in the place.' Using my own words, I would say the garden is not a passive 'field of experience' awaiting your enjoyment; it is not 'going on' for you. In fact, you are one of the myriad things going on in the garden. It is as if there really is a presence, a spirit of the place appointed to watch over the garden, as the Romans believed. In this encounter, the spirit is fulfilling its duty to protect the place from preconceived expectations, or from complacency. You could imagine the presence pushes back, testing you, to remind you that, in this place, you are not the center of things. The garden is the thing.

You may reject this as hocus-pocus drivel. Being a rationalist, a believer in science, I've felt the same for much of my life—but I've come to realize that it doesn't matter a bit whether I believe in a spirit of the place or not. If I have a feeling, an inner experience, then that experience is as real as a solid rock lying at my feet.

The spirit of the place is real.

MAP OF THE GARDEN The map shows the garden in its woodland context, surrounded by forest, its multiple intersecting pathways, and its significant areas and features.

0 | Main entrance

1 | Woodland garden

2 | Cross path

3 | Mud garden

4 | Stone circle

5 | Immersion pathway

6 | Thinking bench

7 | Lower reflecting pool

8 | Terrace

9 | Terrace bench

10 | Canal pond

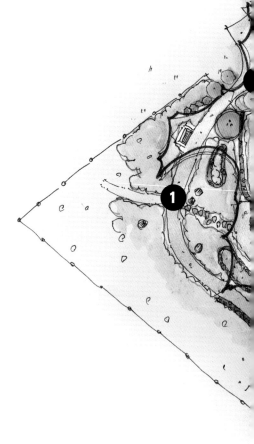

Stopping places

The paths at Federal Twist enable you to explore the landscape, and that exploration takes you by small 'stopping places' where you can pause, perhaps sit and linger, just observe, let your mind go free. It's the nature of the garden that at full growth, the plants hide these quiet, tranquil corners and alcoves, providing cover for human visitors much as wild vegetation gives cover to wildlife. One of the best ways to get a feel for the garden's character and spatial organization is to look at it from several of these refuges, which offer many different viewpoints. The map of the garden along with the brief descriptions and photographs on the next few pages illustrate this.

Woodland

You enter the garden through the woodland and you're immediately plunged into thick vegetation, which is in sharp contrast to the openness just outside the gate. This transition can be a surprise for first-time visitors. You are led along a curving path with partial views into the sunny prairie (though you can't yet see what it is). A bench is to the right, while the path curves left toward the open garden below. If you take time to sit, you have a partial view down gently falling terrain through the trees and woodland shade to the bright center of the garden in the distance.

This shady spot is probably one of the pleasantest places to sit and rest on a hot day, and it's a place of refuge with the merest prospect of the open garden in the distance beyond.

A tupelo (*Nyssa sylvatica*) is one of the most striking plants in the woodland garden because it has suckered profusely, creating its own glade of about 20 smaller trees of various heights around it, one probably almost 20ft (6m) high, and most shaped symmetrically with pointed tops. When the leaves turn light red and orange (not the typical brilliant red) in autumn, the grove of nyssa suckers suggests an array of imaginary Christmas trees. Since this is by far the shadiest part of the garden, the plant composition is a mixture of small trees and shrubs, perennials, and ferns.

Under the tall canopy of the nyssa and several maples, the ground is covered by a variety of foliage plants that create a dark background, shot through by changing points and splashes of light as the sun moves. Here and elsewhere in the garden I've used a mixture of plants of different origins, some native and some not. The primary criterion for selection is, 'Can this plant survive and thrive here?' Walking through the small woodland, you will see several Japanese maples (*Acer japonicum*) in raised stone beds; two airy sweetbay magnolias (*Magnolia virginiana*) by the entrance gate; coastal doghobble (*Leucothoe axillaris*), native low shrubs that perform extremely well in the shade and wet; arrowwood (*Viburnum dentatum*), with such straight stems the Native Americans used them to make arrows; arborvitae (*Thuja occidentalis*); white wood aster (*Eurybia divaricata*), which profusely lines the woodland pathways; hardy begonia (*Begonia grandis*), for a bit of an autumn pink floral surprise; many pulmonaria, all variegated and with early spring flowers changing from blue to pink; autumn fern (*Dryopteris erythrosora* 'Brilliance'); golden ragwort (*Packera aurea*), which covers the ground in gold in late spring; sweet woodruff (*Galium odoratum*), an indigenous ground cover that moves about wherever conditions suit it; *Geranium maculatum*, a native perennial but one that seems to appear and disappear almost at random; woodoats (*Chasmanthium latifolium*), for its striking autumn seed heads; *Hosta* species; *Phlox divaricata* 'Blue Moon'; Christmas fern (*Polystichum acrosticoides*); ostrich fern (*Matteuccia struthiopteris*); black snakeroot (*Sanicula odorata*); horsetail (*Equisetum arvense*); occasional odd exotics such as *Cacalia delphinifolia*, and a variety of carex.

LEFT Views of the woodland garden.

The cross path

As you continue down the main path for a couple of hundred feet (60m), you will come to another bench at the intersection with the oldest path across the garden. A river birch (*Betula nigra* HERITAGE) provides shade and through its drooping branches allows a view toward the center of the garden. This is a pleasant entry point to the prairie garden, particularly in spring and early summer. By midsummer, however, the plants are so large you can't see far. This is a point where you make a decision to cross the garden or continue along the main path toward the back. Being a busy person, I find this a bit frustrating, even annoying at times, but different routes can provide different rewards depending on weather and season. Most people want to see the garden in the most direct and efficient way, but that isn't possible. I have to slow down, even though I already know what is ahead (sometimes I'm surprised), perhaps linger a few moments, then go one way or the other, and let the garden take control.

I garden this center path through summer mostly by subtraction, because our frequent and violent thunderstorms often leave tall plants leaning across the way. It's ordinarily a quick matter to remove them, but storms on the wrong day can be a major inconvenience. So I've gradually added more shrubs and small trees— chokeberry (*Aronia arbutifolia* 'Brilliantissima'), sweetbay magnolia (*Magnolia virginiana*), spicebush (*Lindera benzoin)*, doublefile viburnum (*Viburnum plicatum*

LEFT AND BELOW The entrance gate to the woodland garden (left) and the main path as it leaves the woodland garden (below).

f. *tomentosum* 'Mariesii'), button bush (*Cephalanthus occidentalis*), a dwarf weeping nyssa, which can't fall, and more will probably follow. I'm also experimenting with *Carex crinita*, the largest of our native carex, as one visually pleasing way to keep tall plants away from the path edge. The cross path comes into its most characterful phase in spring, when it gives a wide overview of the low, emerging, highly decorative foliage, and in late autumn and winter, when its relative openness gives views into the surrounding tall plants as they color, die, and begin to disintegrate into abstract forms.

The mud garden

This area, immediately adjacent to the property line and the unmanaged woodland, was almost an afterthought. I first thought it would be a corner of the prairie garden and assumed I'd eventually get to it. But it didn't want to be that, and it bothered me until I felt I had to give it attention. It turned out to be its own unique place. I discovered it is an observatory, a place to linger and take in the view, especially in spring, but the name 'observatory' seems too sophisticated for such a simple (and admittedly rather messy) place, so I decided to call it the mud garden.

The name is a joke. A small ditch, probably 1ft (30cm) wide and 8in (20cm) deep at most, runs from the side of the house across the end of the prairie garden, into the woods. This spot originally appeared to be appropriate for water-loving plants; however, it never quite lived up to that billing, at least not in droughty summers. I recently planted a katsura (*Cercidiphyllum japonicum*), which should dramatically increase shading and, as it matures, bring other qualities to this place.

BELOW On a spring afternoon, the mud garden is a magnificent place to observe the abundant planting of the prairie, rising like a tide, with shafts of late sunlight streaming across it.

THE VIEW FROM FEDERAL TWIST

It's a quite pleasant spot, with five log seats in a circle and plants that like moist conditions along the little channel—*Rodgersia pinnata*, *Darmera peltata*, various water irises including an unusual Louisiana iris named 'Black Gamecock' (*Iris louisiana* 'Black Gamecock'), ostrich fern (*Matteuccia struthiopteris*), cinnamon fern (*Osmunda cinnamomea*), royal fern (*Osmunda regalis*), sensitive fern (*Onoclea sensibilis*), button bush (*Cephalanthus occidentalis*), Joe Pye weed (*Eupatorium maculatum*), astilbe, various carex, aronia and numerous other moisture-loving plants.

You see striking views at twilight in spring and early summer, when you raise your eyes and look out across the prairie garden toward the house, to the large sycamores (*Platanus occidentalis*) rising above it and the woodland garden. The view is west, so late in the afternoon rays of sunlight stream through. Especially in spring, it's a pleasant place to linger and observe the chiaroscuro effects of light and shade moving over the garden. Suspended above, as if signaling its location, is the Calderesque mobile, consisting of five diminishing red circles that slowly turn in the breeze.

The stone circle

A somber, gray stone called argillite is abundant here—most conveniently piled into rough stone rows by early settlers as they cleared the land for agricultural purposes—and this I eventually used to make a large stone circle. Argillite has become part of the local culture, and I use it to amplify the character of the place. The stones make a ringing sound when hit together, so a very early and still current name is 'blue jingle' or 'blue jingler'.

I never intended the stone circle to have any utilitarian purpose. It exists simply as a place to linger and see a view of the garden not available elsewhere, as a way to intensify the character and atmosphere of the place, and to prod the imagination.

RIGHT A bit of diversion. This Calderesque mobile moves in and out of visibility where it hangs and turns in the breeze above the mud garden. If it were a bit more prominent, I'd probably take it down, but it's a pleasant ornament, especially in autumn.

BELOW The stone circle is the largest structure in the garden. It's made of a hard local mudstone called argillite ('blue jingle' in the local argot, because the stones ring when hit together) that is ubiquitous in this area. Here the circle is like a plant dam, preventing spillover of the prairie into one of the few open spaces in the garden. Like the rest of the garden, it has absolutely no utility. It exists to add visual weight, atmosphere, and to serve as a stopping place, perhaps to sit, observe, or let your mind wander.

The circle gives a view across the garden early in the season, but by midsummer the view is blocked by tall, thickly growing prairie and the interest shifts to closeup observation of the plants. I added a fire pit soon after the circle was completed, but the thought of actually sitting there around a fire was too suggestive of the suburban backyard, so I removed it.

Let's say it's for magic.

Its creation is an example of how the slow accretion of ideas over several years can offer a solution to a problem you didn't know existed. On a visit long ago, Carrie Preston, an American garden designer friend living in the Netherlands, suggested that I use more stone in the garden since I had so much readily available. I had already built several hundred feet of stone wall, and I didn't want to make some arbitrary stone structure that wouldn't belong, so I let the suggestion rest for quite a while. By 2014, three Japanese fantail willows (*Salix udensis* 'Sekka') I had planted along a curve in the main back path had grown into substantial small trees with large, twisted trunks. At that point, the circle simply came to mind as an aesthetically appropriate object to rest under those trees, at the edge across the prairie garden, opposite the house. Pretty much on a whim, I asked Milton and his father to make the circle just before winter.

BELOW Here is another reason for the stone circle—as a focal point for the brown and gold grasses of winter, and as a reminder of senescence, death, and rebirth.

I call it simply a 'stone circle' and I'm not happy to hear others refer to it as a 'council ring'. I want visitors to relate directly to the argillite stone circle in my garden, and to evoke Jens Jensen and all the historical and cultural associations of his 'council ring' introduces information that, to my mind, interferes with the immediate experience of this place. To me, it's a bit akin to calling a pond a 'water feature'. That 'alien' term evokes a different part of the country, a distant, more Midwestern culture. It comes between the visitor and a direct experience of this place. Not every stone circle is necessarily a council ring.

The circle is the most massive structure in the garden, so it is an especially notable feature during autumn, winter, and spring, when it is more easily seen from a distance. The garden's autumn and winter colors also highlight the dark, somber, hardness of the stone and give it added weight in the landscape—not just visual power, but a 'felt' presence.

Both the circle and the adjacent mud garden, also with its own circle of log seats, can suggest a sense of some ancient ritual, especially as twilight fades into darkness. The symbol of the circle as a meeting place in the garden evokes questions of what such imaginary meetings might be for.

The immersion pathway

The word knowledgeable visitors probably use most frequently to characterize my garden is 'immersive'. It certainly is that, so you'll probably understand why I sometimes imagine the garden, especially as darkness approaches, as a garden under the ocean, immersed literally.

Out in the open garden, I long ago made a wide, paved path through the middle of the prairie, at that time the largest open area in the garden. My plan was to interrupt the prairie, to divide it into two parts that might develop differently. Without this interruption, 80–90 percent of the garden would be impassible, so

BELOW LEFT Wave Hill chairs on the immersion path while the surrounding growth is low—rigid structure amid rising wildness.

BELOW RIGHT The immersion path from above in autumn, with two Wave Hill chairs in place. Most of the plants along the path are above head height.

adding this path also created another way to experience the garden. In early spring, the path is anything but immersive, but this flat view lasts only a month or so.

I positioned two Wave Hill chairs here (my chairs are actually a modified design made by Dan Benarcik of Chanticleer). Their modernist, sculptural presence offers a striking contrast to the low, almost baroque tapestry of plants in spring and early summer.

This is a pleasant place to sit out and enjoy the emerging vegetation in spring and early summer before the plants attain their ultimate height and close off the open view. By midsummer, the chairs are buried deeply within an abundance of tall miscanthus, silphium, vernonia, and other plants. You can still sit here, enjoy the detail of the plantings, and perhaps talk in solitude with a friend, but the feeling has changed dramatically. You are immersed and when you want to see more of the garden, you must stand up and move.

But to leave the impression this path is only for observation and sitting is to tell just part of the story. The path is also for entertainment, a place for ornament, like a trill or a grace note in a Bach organ fugue. The rigid structure of the two Wave Hill chairs amid tumultuous spring growth is akin to musical ornamentation.

ABOVE Since the prairie is the largest part of the garden, and there was no way to enter it to see it up close, I made a wide, curving path across the garden, dividing the prairie into two unequal parts. The path is a place to sit and observe the plants. As you can see, when the plants are low, it serves admirably. However, as large perennials grow up around it, by midsummer it becomes more a corridor than a pathway, so I've come to call it the immersion path. Though blocked from entering the prairie, you can see through the tall plants into the it on both sides. I think this constraint on visibility and access actually makes immersion in the details of the prairie more powerful.

The Wave Hill chair has an interesting history. In 1960, the American landscape architect Lester Collins, who designed Innisfree—one of the great American landscape gardens—adapted a modernist chair, originally designed in 1918 by Dutch architect Gerrit Rietveld, for use in the garden. The chairs have also been used at Wave Hill, a notable garden overlooking the Hudson River in the northern tip of New York City, for many decades, and thus have become informally known as Wave Hill chairs. Others, notably Dan Benarcik of Chanticleer garden near Philadelphia, have adapted the design, and it is becoming more widely available in the USA. 🌿

The thinking bench

The place I call the thinking bench is at a rear corner of the garden, where I placed a wooden bench on a low paved plinth beneath an old red maple (*Acer rubrum*). The bench is backed by a formal corner hedge of hornbeam (*Carpinus betulus*) and surrounded by paniculate hydrangeas and a wedge of self-seeded inula. The hornbeam hedge has long and short arms, at right angles, so you feel enclosed and protected. As a formal element in a very naturalistic garden, the

hedge brings the garden space to a full stop at that corner, until you realize even that barrier is permeable, and you can walk around the end into a wilder part of the garden where I place extra plants without making a full commitment to defining it as 'garden'. For some reason, I like to leave it as an 'undefined', 'in-between' space that I may or may not finish someday. As in most parts of the garden, views out are open early in the year, but become close, and private, by summer. This corner is certainly the most 'enclosed' place in the garden. Sitting here, you are hidden from view. I sometimes sit there with a cup of coffee in the

ABOVE The place I call the thinking bench is a very private place—you're hidden sitting there. A bench on a paved plinth is backed by an L-shaped hornbeam hedge, making it the most formal part of the garden.

morning. Even on hot days, air drifts in from the surrounding shady forest and I can feel the coolness against my skin.

Because this place is so private, it's ideal for intimate moments. Several years ago I reconnected with a 'lost' high school friend with whom I'd had quite a close relationship. We hadn't seen each other for more than 45 years, and getting together again aroused a jumble of emotions. When he visited, we naturally gravitated to the bench in that private corner to talk about our relationship many years in the past. It was quite an emotional time for me, and this was the perfect place for our exploration of the past, of what might have been lost, and our feelings then.

The reflecting pool

The bank that runs down from the east end of the terrace had always obscured the view of the area immediately below. As a consequence, I neglected it for several years. One day, walking through that 'vacant' area, it occurred to me that a reflecting pool could add interest to the garden, provide an opportunity for a new 'place' with new views out, and functionally link together unconnected parts of the garden, creating a richer experience. So I drew a rough diagram to guide

BELOW The reflecting pool sits at the bottom of the bank descending from the terrace. It is not visible from the terrace and is only occasionally visible from other parts of the garden. This is a tranquil spot for sitting and scanning the broken view out through a screen of perennials, grasses, and shrubs. The sides of the pool are aligned with the four points of the compass. Here the right edge faces north.

Milton and his father, ordered several tons of gravel, and asked them to start moving large stones to make a rock and gravel platform into which we would build a simple reflecting pool.

Because the house and entire garden are, in a sense, 'cut loose' from any sense of direction, other than the path of the sun, and because the Delaware River curves around the area (you can point any direction in a 180 degree curve and you are pointing toward the river), it's not easy to get an accurate fix on direction. I used a compass to align the sides of the pool with the four points of the compass, giving visitors one way to connect with the much wider landscape and understand the garden's orientation on the 'globe' of Earth I think we all carry in our heads.

The pool area has a view up the bank, which is filled with miscanthus, inula, and petasites, to a tall, multi-stemmed snag, a former Japanese weeping cherry that I had cut into a rough sculpture after it died. The snag is now rather gothic, towering high above the terrace and the garden below. It is rotting and will someday fall, but I'll keep it as long as possible. It's a significant presence in the garden, like a totem god set there to oversee the place, and it's beneficial to wildlife. Two more Wave Hill chairs offer seating by the pool and broken views across the pool through surrounding trees and shrubs.

The pool can be glimpsed from other parts of the garden, but it isn't always clear how to get to it. I have given thought to making the approach easier to negotiate, but have as yet resisted doing that. I see this as another way the garden can push back a bit and ask you to find your way through.

ABOVE At ground level, you usually catch only transient glimpses of the reflecting pool through openings in the surrounding plantings.

ABOVE This short stairway up to the terrace from the garden carries you into the shade of three large sycamores (*Platanus occidentalis*), then to a paved area with four Adirondack chairs, and a small, rectangular reflecting pool at the sunny end. The brightly lit plants by the stairway are *Aralia cordata* 'Sun King' and *Kirengeshoma palmata*.

The terrace

The house was built on an earthen berm that elevates it above the wet ground, so it overlooks the garden from a height. An irregular gravel terrace about 20ft (6m) in width extends along the entire length of the house, providing ample space for sitting out, having drinks, or just passing the time. Immediately outside the window wall of the living room is slate paving with a low table and four Adirondack chairs looking out toward the garden. This is the only place for sitting out as a group.

Because the house is raised and the garden wraps about it, almost hiding it from below, the terrace is a refuge and for most of the year a principal viewing place for the garden and the sky. Only from the terrace are you able to comfortably see the drama of a cloudy, stormy sky, the moon, and the stars. In the green summer, however, the terrace takes on a dual aspect: one end is sunny, and the rest is shaded by three large sycamores (*Platanus occidentalis*), providing ample opportunity for both sun and shade planting. At the sunny end I recently added a second, smaller reflecting pool. This new pool gives the terrace a visual 'off-center' focal point that intensifies the change in character between the sunny and shaded parts of the terrace. And introducing water here has brought new life, creating a mirror for the sky and encouraging aquatic life (mainly frogs) up to the driest part of the garden.

Plants surrounding the pool block the view into the garden beyond. Many of these are opaque, mounded shapes—grasses mostly—that become lighter in late summer to autumn when the perennials flower and the grasses put up their feathery wands. Several other perennials and smaller grasses—*Sanguisorba officinalis* 'Red Thunder', *Patrinia scabiosifolia*, *Asclepias tuberosa*, *Baptisia australis*, *Chasmanthium latifolium*, *Panicum virgatum* 'Cape Breeze'—add visual diversity immediately around the pool.

The bank down to the garden is thickly planted with grasses on the sunny side and more shade-tolerant plants—various hydrangeas, *Lindera benzoin*, *Aconitum carmichaelii*, rodgersia, aralia, hakonechloa—at the shady end. The edge of the terrace is planted with a variety of hostas, masses of self-seeded stinking hellebores (*Helleborus foetidus*) that dramatically flower in close view of the living room in mid-winter, *Heuchera villosa* 'Autumn Bride', *Hakonechloa macra*, *Packera aurea*, and a number of geophytes including *Colchicum autumnale* and a variety of allium, crocus, galanthus and other small bulbs. The evergreen *Helleborus foetidus* is especially striking in autumn and winter when everything else is either underground or a shade of brown.

Billowy plantings along the terrace and big leafy limbs hanging down from the sycamores frame some views of the lower garden while blocking others—a kind of hide-and-seek playfulness that gives the garden below some mystery. You have to walk around to get a sense of what is down there. These informal, fractal-like

ABOVE LEFT In this shady view of the center terrace, you can just see four Adirondack chairs lined up in front of the window wall.

ABOVE RIGHT Flowers of *Kolkwitzia amabilis* 'Maradco' DREAM CATCHER on the terrace.

RIGHT Further along the terrace, toward its sunny eastern end, this small rectangular reflecting pool makes an elegant contrast with the surrounding naturalistic plantings. The juxtaposition of the sharply defined pool, the repeated domes of miscanthus, and the flowing vegetation give this part of the garden a 'designed' look not typical of the garden as a whole.

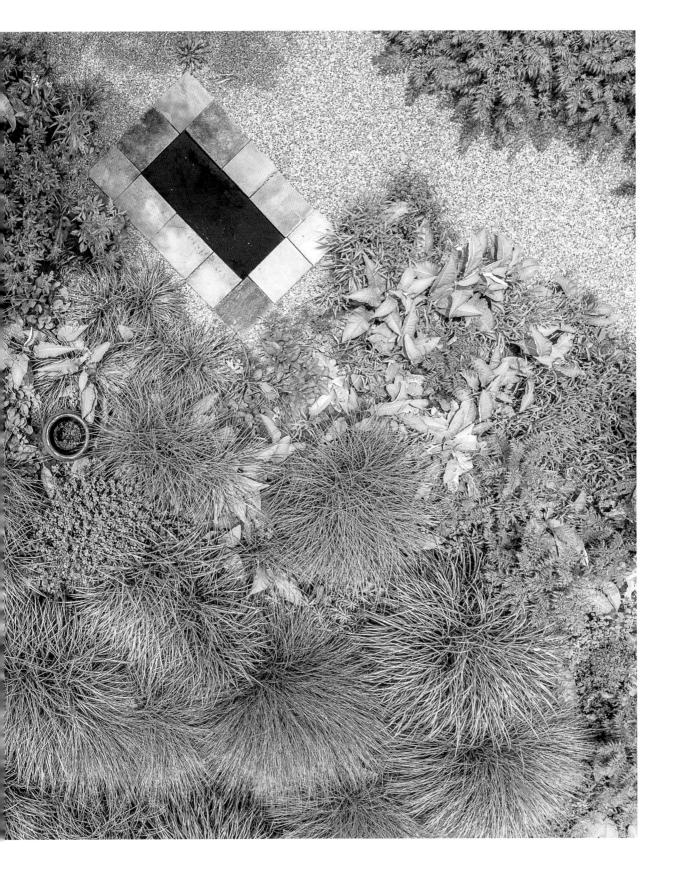

framing devices near the house are mirrored by patterns and textures in horizontal layers of plants and shrubs in the mid-distance, and large trees beyond, creating the illusion of greater depth across the garden and making it seem larger than it is.

When on the terrace, you are wrapped in vegetation. A large mass of cut-leaf sumac (*Rhus glabra* 'Laciniata') occupies almost a third of the length of the house at one end, requiring a cut back each year. It's part of several broken layers of planting along the terrace and the ends of the house. They make the house seem a bit mysterious when viewed from out in the garden.

The terrace bench

At the south end of the terrace is a simple bench made of square concrete blocks as the base with two boards across. The design is very much of the 1960s era and is a visual reminder of the period of the house. It's all quite simple but that corner of the terrace catches long shadows around sunset, turning a quiet corner into a place of awe. From the bench in the low light, you have an inward view notable only because it's not particularly notable. A *Fargesia rufa* bamboo and *Heptacodium miconioides* are across the terrace, to the left is a *Chionanthus virginicus* underplanted by *Kirengeshoma palmata*, and across are several large hostas.

Next to the hostas is one of three *Lindera angustifolia* var. *glabra* extending back in an uneven line; these screen the narrow end of the house from the woodland garden. They are attractive shrubs and will become small multistem trees with time. Their importance relative to the terrace bench, however, is what happens in autumn. The shrubs always make a theatrical show of color, sometimes changing to bright orange, or bright red, or turning multiple colors on the same shrub, even on individual leaves—pink, yellow, orange, purple, and all finally turning brown. They remain on the shrub until spring when they are pushed off by the emerging foliage.

The canal pond

The largest of the three water bodies in the garden, the canal pond is intended to echo the canals along both sides of the Delaware, built by Irish immigrant laborers in the 1830s. The canals were important for transportation and commerce along the river and, as rail replaced them, they became important recreational resources. Their history has influenced the area for almost two centuries and they still contribute to making it a center for weekend getaways and tourism. They are so important culturally, I felt they deserved a symbolic bow.

To control cost, I had to keep an eye out for the most efficient use of available materials; the pond came to me by chance. When Milton and his father had

BELOW The canal pond recalls the canals built along both sides of the Delaware by Irish immigrant laborers in the 1830s. When overgrown with vegetation, as here, people often think it is actually a running stream.

completed a 200ft (60m) dry-laid stone wall around the base of the house embankment, they pointed to the vacant space behind it. We needed a lot of soil as fill.

Since most of the rainwater flows around the southerly end of the house, I suggested they dig a pond there so the water would flow naturally into it, and that they use the excavated soil to fill in behind the wall. I had them make the pond long and narrow, so it would resemble the historic canals along the Delaware. I know the canal allusion works; when the pond edge is fully vegetated, many people mistake it for a stream.

Though the two much smaller reflecting pools have frogs in them, the canal pond is the center of aquatic life in the garden. On some spring and summer nights, the strange, almost primeval sound of the frogs and spring peepers is so loud, you might think you were in the jungles of South America.

The main access to the pond is by a path below the terrace, which passes along the length of the pond then winds out into the central garden, where it connects with other paths. Alternatively, once at the pond, you can turn right and take a simple wooden bridge, stand above the water and enjoy the view, then walk on along a secondary path made of black locust (*Robinia pseudoacacia*) rounds, passing through a massive petasites field to another main path.

Memory

Memory believes before knowing remembers. Believes longer than recollects, longer than knowing even wonders.

William Faulkner, *Light in August*

I will always remember one special day in the garden. This happened in the very early years when I was actually working in it.

The last day of summer: I was at the back of the garden, far away from the house, surrounded by a mess of still wildish vegetation, sweating, in a kind of dreamy state from the heat. I was trying to tie up some storm-tossed Indian grass so it looked reasonably natural. Squatting. Brushing the bugs away. Cutting twine and tying. It was the tying that was the gift into memory and imagination. I was engaged in a simple physical way with a problem in the world. Twilight was darkening into evening. Not quiet, insect sounds all around. Buzzing, whirring, the rhythmic vocalizations of frogs.

I had been thinking about the people who had farmed the land where I was making my garden— thinking how hard their lives must have been, struggling with the rocky earth to grow crops on difficult land.

In my imagination, possibly a bit confused, I merged these people with my own agrarian ancestors, remembering a memory I never had. Since my mother's recent death, I had been tracing my ancestry and had discovered that after some early ancestors arrived on the New England shores in 1620, nearly all

their subsequent descendants, all the way down to my grandparents' generation, had spent their lives as poor, subsistence, 'dirt' farmers. They slowly moved southward down the East Coast, generation after generation, as lands were cleared of Native Americans and made available for white settlers (yet another sad story), then turned westward across Georgia, to Alabama, to Mississippi, and to former Choctaw land, where I was born.

I thought of my great-great-grandfather, seeing him as a symbol of the generations of farmers I am descended from. This little action, tying up wild grasses, was like one of the many simple acts of survival my ancestors had been carrying out through the centuries. Squatting inelegantly in my garden, wanting to finish before the rain, I thought of him.

In the moment of digging in the darkening twilight, I had a kind of waking dream—my actions became one with those of my great-great-grandfather back in Mississippi in the 1870s, struggling in rhythm with me, across time and space, tediously unwinding twine, tying up dry grasses, trying to get something done.

Two times, two places, become one. 🌿

PLANTING
THE
GARDEN

Science now knows with theoretical certainty . . .
that the first sparks of life—the first primitive cells
with membranes containing RNA—occurred within
common clay minerals . . . which provided the basic
platforms for the formation, growth, and division
of some of the earliest living cells on Earth.
In the beginning there was clay.

Robert Pogue Harrison, *Gardens: An Essay on the Human Condition*

ABOVE The garden is born of the ecology of its site and this white heath aster (*Symphyotrichum ericoides*) is indigenous to the site. It remains inconspicuous until autumn, when it flowers in bushy masses.

I admired the gardens of Piet Oudolf and that was the kind of garden I thought I wanted had it been possible. However, I quickly learned my approach would have to be entirely different. An Oudolf garden would start with a clean slate, carefully prepared land, and crews planting thousands of small plug plants to an exact design plan. After a long period of establishment and care, the intention would be for the mature garden to retain its designed form. This wasn't a method that could meet my needs in any practical way, certainly not without great expense, considering my heavy clay soil, which would be the ultimate arbiter in plant selection. Also, I would need to plant large to outcompete and dominate much of the weedy vegetation on my site.

Other issues for me, I came to discover, were personal preference and, to a certain degree, comfort. I wanted a much looser planting concept, and—unlike Oudolf—I learned I wanted my plants to move about; that's the nature of this wildish place. I knew I'd enjoy the engagement with the garden that spontaneity would foster.

Federal Twist is born of the ecology of its site, very much in the tradition of Gilles Clément's 'garden in movement'. Clément, a French landscape designer with a philosophical bent, not nearly so well known as Piet Oudolf in the English-speaking world, gave a talk on the *jardin en mouvement* in Manhattan in 2013, when my own garden was still in its early days. I attended not knowing what to expect, having never read his books, and was delighted to hear in his talk a concept similar to my own approach to garden-making, as well as a similar understanding of plant communities in movement.

In *Planetary Gardens*, Clément wrote: 'the Garden in Movement interprets and develops the energies found in the place, and attempts to work as much as possible with, and as little as possible against, nature. Its name refers to the physical movement of plant species on the land, which the gardener interprets in his own way... These principles disrupt the formal conception of the garden that, in this case, is totally entrusted to the hands of the gardener. The design of the garden, which constantly changes, is the result of the work of the person who maintains it, not of an idea developed at the drawing board.'

This is a concise description of my own wish to garden in the spirit of the place, to accept the ecology given me, and to set myself the task of participating in a process of constant change, allowing nature or chance to have a say. Of course, my garden design never got to that 'drawing board-stage' Clément mentioned. As I've noted, I approached making the garden as an 'interweaving' of the new with the old; I was working 'in the moment' and was open to new plants seeding in and existing plants moving about. Every act of planting was provisional in nature, subject to change, either intentionally or by some random action.

A time of provisional planting

From the start, planting was an experiment and it remains so today. I think some plants will stay as they are, but the garden is always open to change, whether accidental or planned, even to adjusting to disaster, which comes from time to time.

A central aim has always been to achieve and maintain a certain level of complexity, so I guard against allowing individual species to become too dominant and I add 'disruptors' by such means as broadcasting seed or adding new plants I know will contribute their own seed. Of course, this means the garden remains a moving target, so to speak. I have to pay attention.

In addition to keeping the garden vital, complexity has other purposes. Many studies have demonstrated that spatially complex and diverse plant communities as well as a range of habitats are necessary to support broad diversity in wildlife species, especially invertebrates, whose populations are rapidly declining. My garden is essentially woodland edge habitat, with many variations in moisture, light, and shade, and areas of wild habitat directly adjacent to the gardened areas facilitating movement of wildlife from one to the other. Within the immediate area of the garden and surrounding woods, you will encounter wet, dark woodland, sunny expanses of light, and higher and lower elevations, depending on your position on the gradual slope that is the 'ground' (speaking both philosophically and literally) of the garden.

A word about native plants. While the American enthusiasm for native plants has important benefits—most importantly support of native invertebrates that co-evolved with specific plants essential to their survival—as well as the added benefit of an expanding interest in gardening that has taken place by popularizing use of native plants—the exclusive focus of many landscape architects, garden designers, ecologists, horticulturists, and governmental entities responsible for planting public spaces has resulted in a narrowing of vision and a flattening of the aesthetic and moral potential of gardens. For those interested in the ecological benefits of gardening, it's important to be aware that complex, highly diverse, layered plantings using many different species are extremely valuable, even if not all native. Added to this are the many changes in plant habitat and distribution occurring because of climate change; what is native in one place today may not be native in another decade. We are now living in a time when all our ecosystems have already been changed by the activities of human beings, and the speed of change will only accelerate with climate change. Species introduced from other parts of the world will never be completely extirpated. We must now learn how to live with novel ecosystems, and it's essential we learn to manage them rather than hoping to take nature back to some 'pristine' moment in time before humans started moving plants around the world.

But to return to the subject of complexity, complexity of structure and composition are static concepts with little meaning until we consider them over time. It is important to use plants that flower at different times to provide food for pollinators throughout the growing season, for example. Of course, a part of achieving complex biodiversity is the use of native plants whenever possible, though I by no means limit my plant palette to natives. I also allow plants to seed in by chance and, if I like them, and they are in good positions, I accept and try to manage them, at least for a while. And I use non-natives when appropriate, for aesthetic reasons alone.

BELOW All my planting is provisional and subject to change. Luck, chance, accident all have roles to play. About *Silphium laciniatum*, one thing is a certainty: when it grows tall enough, it will fall over. This is what we see here—a spire of *Silphium laciniatum* become horizontal, against a prairie background.

ABOVE The plants in the garden are provisional, temporary, ever-changing. Ironically, all the plants on this page, though provisional, have always been in the garden, either because they are indigenous to the place or they have seeded in from somewhere nearby and found an appropriate ecological niche. Clockwise from top left: Deptford pink (*Dianthus armeria*), seedbox (*Ludwigia alternifolia*), dogbane (*Apocynum cannabinum*) seed pods, an unidentified carex (I have many), and *Apocynum cannabinum* in flower.

My first significant planting sprang out of a sudden impulse after I mowed that first path across the raw garden space. I had recently seen a large number of *Filipendula rubra* 'Venusta' in large pots at a local nursery and knew they would make an effective long drift of big perennials. While some of my plantings were carefully planned, many early plantings were a result of such impulse buys. Because sufficient numbers of appropriate plants were simply not available to me, I had to take plants as I found them. I was working in New York City, making a garden in the country on weekends, and did not have access to wholesale 'to-the-trade-only' nurseries, so I often toured retail nurseries on weekends, searching willy-nilly, depending on chance to find plants. I'll never forget my delight when I found a cache of *Rudbeckia maxima*. However, during most of these rather rambling searches, I was looking for specific plants; I had a design process in mind, if not a design plan on paper. If I had *Rudbeckia maxima* in the ground already, I kept my eye open for more so that I could use it to build the design; if I found a source of *Miscanthus* 'Purpurascens', I looked for more so I could develop complementary groupings in different parts of the garden. I also used my gardening blog to do a lot of 'thinking out loud' as planting proceeded, and

solicited comments and conversations with many readers, which I'm sure played a role in making the garden what it is today.

My intention was to establish plant communities, not to plant individual specimen plants. As a working definition, I envisioned a plant community as a group of plants that are compatible with each other and the site, and composed of different vertical layers of vegetation, so constituted that they grow and can be cared for as a visually unified community.

It is important to understand that 'plant community' implies only proximity and compatibility, not some kind of 'mystical' unity. As Rainer and West state: 'Plant communities are human constructs, conceptual frames for describing a group of plants in a place … These communities do not exist in nature as distinct organisms … [they are] made up of groups of overlapping populations that coexist and interact. Plant communities are an abstraction, a naming convention we use to describe vegetation so we can study it.'

In working with plants growing in community, garden care is more like agriculture than traditional horticultural gardening practice. Plants are managed as groups, not as individuals, so an understanding of how plants function

ABOVE Early on I planted a broad sweep of *Filipendula rubra* 'Venusta' in what was to become my novel prairie. That original planting has remained very stable over many years. In the photograph above, you can see how thickly the filipendula is emerging. It appears to have arranged itself into roughly three large circular areas (more are off to the right of the picture). It resists incursion by other plants very well, but I'm certain it isn't permanent and, some day, I'll need to deal with change. The meaning of 'provisional' is relative.

communally is essential. For example, herbaceous species that are large and tall occupy the top layer and normally require higher levels of light, mid-level species can tolerate more shade and grow among tall species in larger groups, and below all of them ground-cover species occupy the lowest layer. These are normally small plants that cover the soil at the base of taller species, and they are the most shade-tolerant ones. Many other variables affect plants growing in community, of course, such as plant sociability, tolerance of competition, root structure, mechanisms for spreading laterally, foliage size and shape, light requirements, availability of water, a variety of environmental conditions, and other factors. Since I wanted a kind of wet prairie, I of course wanted prairie plants, but

RIGHT Miscanthus surrounding a group of tall *Rudbeckia maxima*. This photo flips the idea of designing with ground cover, mid-level, and tall emergent plants on its head. In a more traditional garden, both the miscanthus and rudbeckia would be considered tall emergents, but here the miscanthus really functions in three ways—as a ground cover, though a very tall one, as a matrix plant and, especially when in flower, as a tall emergent. In this case, the *Rudbeckia maxima* functions as a tall emergent simply because it's visually very distinctive. The labels, like the plants, are merely provisional and will change as the planting grows and evolves.

I couldn't find sources for most of them. I could have obtained small plants from nurseries in the Midwest, but small plants did not have a good record of survival in my competitive emerging prairie. So I decided to give seeding a try. I ordered seed of cup plant (*Silphium perfoliatum*) and compass plant (*S. laciniatum*) and broadcast it in the autumn. I didn't see any plants the following year, but they did begin to emerge in the second year. I couldn't find seed for prairie dock (*S. terebinthinaceum*) but I did obtain bare root plants, which were successful. Today, of course, I have more than enough of all the silphiums so I pull out what I don't want.

Did I mention I also garden by subtraction?

RIGHT The immense size of some of the tall perennials creates a 'wow' factor in high summer. These images hardly do justice to the swirl of yellow flowers surrounding you and waving against the sky in mid- to late July. Shown here are mostly *Silphium perfoliatum* and *Hemerocallis altissima*, which peak in this season, though other plants are important in this phase.

ABOVE The emerging plant matrix shortly after it has broken the soil surface and started to grow: *Filipendula rubra* 'Venusta', *Onoclea sensibilis*, *Euphorbia palustris*, *Equisetum arvense*, *Inula racemosa* 'Sonnenspeer', and a few solidago.

Modified matrix planting

Making the garden began with experimental planting in 2005, and my early design efforts focused on planting perennials and grasses in the large, roughly oval area that was to become a wet prairie—albeit an imaginary prairie unlike any that ever existed in New Jersey. Some decisions were purely aesthetic (what I thought would be visually appropriate), some were based on ecological conditions (was it wet enough for plant A, or sunny enough for plant B?), and some were intended to promote biodiversity.

Using current terminology, I made what could be called a modified matrix planting using a mixture of grasses and herbaceous perennials to cover the ground at low to mid-levels. I use the word matrix to identify a typology of planting, where species which share similar environmental needs are planted in random layout and are allowed to interact with each other rather than being grouped in rigid blocks of single species. I say 'modified' matrix because I believe my method differs from the usual, relying less on planting and more on random, cumulative effects of natural growth, spread, and seeding over a period of years (similar to Gilles Clément's concept of the garden in movement). My aim was to create a designed plant community that would thrive in my conditions and feel appropriate to the wild character of the place.

ABOVE As growth advances, the *Euphorbia palustris* has come into flower and the *Onoclea sensibilis* is overtopping the filipendula. This won't last, however, as the filipendula will vastly exceed the height of the onoclea at maturity.

LEFT As growth continues, plant forms further differentiate, and greater diversity becomes apparent. The rough, spade-shaped leaves of *Silphium terebinthinaceum* emerge, clumps of hemerocallis become visible. The grey, slightly succulent foliage of *Rudbeckia maxima* takes form.

Taller, more visually prominent emergents rise higher as summer progresses. I use these two terms—matrix and emergent—only because they are the accepted terminology for meadow and prairie plantings and are useful in describing how the garden is put together; however, the distinction between the matrix layer and the emergent layer becomes rather fuzzy as the garden matures, and the designation of some large, tall plants as matrix plants or emergents becomes largely immaterial.

The ground-cover layer of indigenous plants mostly disappeared as the planting became so dense the lowest layer was shaded out. I've come to think of most of those that remain as a part of the matrix; they include a few tough ground-cover plants such as sensitive fern (*Onoclea sensibilis*), horsetail (*Equisetum arvense*), ragwort (*Packera aurea*), sweet woodruff (*Galium odoratum*), and various carex remaining at the edges.

The plants I chose also tend to blend with other plants to function as a 'seasonal theme layer' (I adopt the term from Rainer and West and use it very loosely), providing flower color, texture, or other visual interest at different times throughout the seasons. They arrange themselves individually and in groups of

various sizes. For example, an irregular cluster of *Miscanthus* 'Purpurascens' might be planted adjacent to a larger array of *Sanguisorba canadensis*, and those might be planted near a scattering of New England asters (*Symphyotrichum novae-angliae*), a group of pink turtlehead (*Chelone lyonii* 'Hot Lips'), or *Hemerocallis* species to provide a burst of color. As I mentioned, I use the term 'seasonal theme layer' quite loosely, so in my garden that layer also includes the most colorful and floriferous plants—those usually termed tall emergents—*Silphium perfoliatum*, *S. laciniatum*, *S. terebinthinaceum*, various *Eupatorium* species, *Vernonia* species, *Filipendula rubra* and *F. ulmaria*, and *Inula racemosa*.

I wanted grasses as a major component of the matrix and, of course, they had to be grasses that could grow in wet soil and less than ideal light conditions. I tried several, but grasses that could perform well in my conditions were few. Following informal and highly unscientific trials, I was left with these: in damp areas, a few *Panicum* such as *P. virgatum* 'Cloud Nine', 'Dallas Blues', 'Northwind', and 'Cape Breeze' (the only panicums I've found that can stand up—for a few years at least—to the competition in the garden), and prairie cordgrass (*Spartina pectinata*). In slightly dryer areas, I also use some *Deschampsia* and *Chasmanthium latifolium*,

CLOCKWISE FROM TOP LEFT
The players—*Sanguisorba
tenuifolia* 'Purpurea', *Apocynum
cannibinum* (dogbane seed heads),
*Iris virginica, Sanguisorba
canadensis, Darmera peltata*
with *Carex muskingumensis.*

and I allow native Indian grass (*Sorghastrum nutans*) to seed where it likes.

But of all these, only miscanthus has proven to work for the long haul. Although it is a Japanese grass, it blends well with my woodland setting and with the house, which has subtle Japanese-influenced features. I use a variety of *Miscanthus* species and cultivars, including *M. sinensis* as the major matrix grass, which has a classic vase shape, the very tall *M. giganteus* for drama and some screening, and *Miscanthus* 'Purpurascens', which has an upright form, much simpler flower heads, and a very good red color in autumn, in contrast to the yellow-gold tones of *M. sinensis* cultivars. I'd love to add *M. nepalensis*, but it isn't hardy in our climate. *Miscanthus sinensis* unfortunately self-seeds quite a bit, but I've compromised on that issue and spend the time necessary to pull out seedlings before they establish themselves. This is mandatory.

Other matrix plants include *Veronicastrum* species which, though slow to gain size in my garden, are durable and slowly grow larger even in highly competitive positions; *Solidago* species, all of which have seeded in from the local area, and some of which are quite aggressive spreaders, so I pull out a lot (they are great late pollinator plants and good for injecting late color); and *Vernonia* of several kinds,

including the giant *V. arkansana* 'Mammuth' (a tall emergent, not a matrix plant, properly speaking). All of the vernonias interbreed and seed themselves to form areas of rich purple in late summer to autumn.

I also grow *Petasites* (mine is a hybrid identified as *P. hybridus* × Dutch with triangular leaves) to try to fulfill my passion for *Gunnera*, which of course can't survive our winters (I discourage others from using this highly invasive plant; only those with the will and means to keep it under control dare plant it); meadowsweet (*Filipendula ulmaria*), which has rather muddy white flowers, but adds a wildish, lacy character to the matrix, growing primarily in a wet area beside the canal pond and seeding itself gently about (though easily removed); and dogbane (*Apocynum cannabinum*), a plant I didn't know that appeared in the garden several years ago. It has the wild look I like, a very loose white umbelliferous flower head, and green bean-like seed pods that open and spill out silky threads after turning brown in late autumn; it both seeds itself and spreads by runners, but I like it enough to go to the trouble of keeping it.

Two favorite components of the matrix—though not a great proportion of it in mass—are rattlesnake master (*Eryngium yuccifolium*), for its foliage and spiky

CLOCKWISE FROM TOP LEFT The players—*Iris ensata* (unnamed), *Hemerocallis* (unnamed), native bracken, *Eupatorium perfoliatum*.

flower head, which looks very unusual for a northeastern garden (though it's native), and a mountain mint (*Pycnanthemum muticum*), which shares its grey color with the eryngium, is exceedingly fragrant, and attracts huge numbers of pollinators.

The Joe Pye weeds (*Eupatorium* or *Eutrochium* spp.) are another favorite, being unusually massive plants with huge umbelliferous flower heads that are magnets for insects. These late risers seem perfectly adapted to my wet conditions, heavy soil and broken light. A notable species I have is *Eupatorium perfoliatum*, which is much smaller, and has white flowers and crinkled, perfoliate leaves. It came into the garden on some anonymous breeze just as I was thinking about digging one from a ditch. It spreads itself gently around and is at its best, I think, in autumn twilight just as it starts to fall apart.

Some plants add bulk to the matrix, while others are more decorative and contribute less to mass. In early spring, the *Euphorbia palustris* makes great mounds of foliage topped by large umbels of glorious golden flowers, then it remains a plant of significant substance throughout the summer, turning to reds, oranges, and yellows in autumn. Flowering in early summer, *Ligularia japonica* plays a similar role, unfolding masses of highly cut foliage, then sending up

CLOCKWISE FROM TOP LEFT
The players—*Hemerocallis altissima*, *Eryngium yuccifolium*, *Aster tartaricus* 'Jin Dai', *Onoclea sensibilis*.

luscious fleshy buds that open to egg-yolk yellow flowers. It tends to grow at the edges of the matrix, and after flowering, it falls apart and flops ungraciously, so I cut much of it out. Other, slimmer plants make different contributions. *Iris virginica* and *I. pseudacorus* have strong structure, which gives them the ability to shoot up through quite dense growth and flower just above the mid-height matrix plants. Hemerocallis, especially *Hemerocallis altissima* cultivars, can do the same, throwing stalks loaded with buds and bright flowers above the mass of growth, then vanishing later in the season.

Some asters do something similar; New England aster (*Symphyotrichum novae-angliae*) can weave itself up through other plants, penetrating the growth almost like a vine, and emerge to flower in autumn just above the other relatively low plants. *Symphyotrichum laeve* 'Bluebird' also manages to thread its way up through thick stems and foliage of *Filipendula rubra* to flower in mid- to late October. Sources tell me it wants full sun and dry soil, so I don't know why it's been growing for years in my garden. And swamp aster (*Symphyotrichum puniceum*) is extremely resilient, having survived many years, and spread easily in one of the most competitive parts of the prairie.

The sanguisorbas are highly distinctive and I do want to add more. I've let the white native *Sanguisorba canadensis* have pretty much free rein to go where it wants, and it has settled into two parts of the prairie. Japanese burnet (*Sanguisorba tenuifolia* 'Purpurea') is a beautiful addition to the prairie, but it does tend to flop without substantial support from other strong plants. If I find *S. tenuifolia* var. *alba* inexpensive enough to purchase in large numbers, I hope to replace many of the 'Purpurea' in the future.

Clearly, this matrix is very different from the typical grassy meadow with seasonal interest plants dropped in singly or grouped. From this unusually tall layer emerge several even larger, taller herbaceous perennials: *Inula racemosa* 'Sonnenspeer', *Rudbeckia maxima*, *Silphium perfoliatum*, *S. laciniatum*, *S. terebinthinaceum*, *Eupatorium purpureum* and *E. maculatum*, *Vernonia arkansana* 'Mammuth', and *Miscanthus giganteus*. Once I understood what large grasses and tall perennials could do, I used their immense size to try to create a 'wow' factor, extending the range of experience possible in a relatively small garden with, by virtue of the wet clay soil, a limited plant selection.

In early spring, when plants start emerging, you can see how the different species in the prairie have organized themselves. The photograph on page 137 shows an area of prairie where I originally planted a mass of *Filipendula rubra*. Although the plants were spaced rather uniformly, they have gradually organized themselves into discernible rings covering the land surface. At the edges of the rings, the foliage of several *Iris pseudacorus* is visible. I think that the iris have created a barrier and had some functional role in shaping the filipendula communities into circles, but that is only speculation. In the foreground is an apparently empty area with just a few visible equisetum. This is actually a large community of *Eupatorium maculatum*, which emerges late but has claimed and maintains its own territory.

This is only a small part of the prairie area. Elsewhere, other plants are still competing for space, as you can see in the lower photograph on page 143 showing emerging filipendula (five-pointed leaves), *Onoclea sensibilis*, *Equisetum arvense*, and solidago, most of which will be pulled out. The onoclea will eventually be shaded out by the taller filipendula, depending on whether I take action to direct events. The filipendula, being taller and larger, has the competitive advantage.

Trees and shrubs

I realized I wanted something to be happening at another level, so I began adding trees and shrubs to enhance diversity and complexity, and to create a physical structure that would add to the character of the landscape throughout the year. I introduced small trees and shrubs—first, and very early in making the garden, three 'Sunburst' honey locusts (*Gleditsia triacanthos* f. *inermis* 'Sunburst') irregularly spaced in a diagonal line across the garden. I wanted them to give a feeling of movement, of procession, and of perspective. Their golden color in spring would complement the gold of *Euphorbia palustris*, *Packera aurea*, and other yellow and gold ground covers, and create a kind of harmonious presence several feet above ground level—a mid-level between the tall trees surrounding the clearing and the lower herbaceous layer.

As I began this process, the garden quickly reminded me that it is a 'garden in movement' (Clément again). Birds, squirrels, the wind were at work too, randomly depositing seed of a variety of trees and shrubs from the surrounding woods. The ground was murmuring with new life rising in unexpected places, so I had to think what I would integrate with the intentional plantings and what I would remove. In fact, most of the interlopers are removed; there are too many. As I was adding layers, each step along that journey was a reminder that the forest was eager, at all times, to swallow the garden. This engenders a profound unease, though one I learned to live with. A simple once-a-year mowing and burning takes care of it. But I was warned, and I would keep watch.

Most of the trees and shrubs I selected I expected to perform well in the wet clay; a few I wasn't sure about. But taking risks, I made some useful discoveries. One of the surprises was the amazing versatility of a very special Asian shrub, *Lindera angustifolia* var. *glabra* (commonly mislabeled *Lindera salicifolia*). I first encountered this lindera at Chanticleer, the public garden near Philadelphia; afterward, I saw it rather massively planted at Brooklyn Bridge Park in Brooklyn; and, as it becomes better known, its use is becoming more prevalent. It has thrived everywhere I've tried it in my garden—in the heavy wet clay of the poorly drained main garden, on a much drier and sunnier bank, at the end of the house elevated by a dry stone wall in dappled shade, and on the side of the house facing Federal Twist Road, in my driest area. Even there, it grows well both in direct sun and in quite shady conditions. This shrub's colors in autumn are extraordinary and quite variable, ranging from yellows to pinks, light purples, oranges, and reds. In some years they are all bright orange. Its shiny black berries form in autumn. This plant is a fast grower in my zone 6b climate; I know it grows into zone 4b in New Hampshire. Another bonus is that deer will not touch it.

I happened to find a rather large seven son flower (*Heptacodium miconioides*) on one of my early plant explorations. I've been fond of this quirky tree since I first saw several large specimens flowering in Bruce Gangewar's Paxson Hill Farm nursery and garden just across the Delaware from me in Pennsylvania. I planted one at the end of the house, where it has grown rapidly in the shade of large sycamores above it. It probably receives at most three hours of partially broken sun each day. It's easy, and takes care of itself. This may be one of my favorite trees, mainly because of its rather awkward, abrupt branching structure, peeling bark, and deeply veined leaves. It's entirely distinctive and though some might consider it to be an ugly duckling, I like its rough, angular, irregular effect in the garden. It does require attention to pruning because of its unusual structure. I later planted two smaller heptacodium in a hedgerow down in the wetter part of the garden, and they are thriving there too, so it seems to be quite tolerant of different soil and light conditions.

Hydrangeas too seem quite variable in their needs. I tried both *Hydrangea paniculata* cultivars and *H. quercifolia* in the wettest part of the garden. To my surprise, the paniculate hydrangeas grew very fast, even in mostly broken shade, and they perform well year after year (with a substantial annual pruning in early spring). However, *H. quercifolia*, by far my favorite, can't survive in the same conditions. I do have one very large *quercifolia* specimen at the end of the house, in drier soil, and it's done very well, growing to about 8 ft (2.4m) high and wide; some others, on the dry shady bank, have developed slowly but not vigorously. So much to my disappointment, I can't grow them with assurance. Cultivars of the native *Hydrangea arborescens* also do well on the bank, but their flowers are too heavy and flop terribly. I'm gradually replacing these with a new patented

arborescens cultivar named 'Haas' Halo', a white lacecap variety that has the strength to hold its flowers erect.

One of the first trees I planted, just inside the entrance gate, was a sweetbay magnolia (*Magnolia virginiana*). I had seen them growing in wet and even flooded areas, so I thought they would make a successful addition to the garden with their open structure, shiny green leaves, and small but beautiful, lemon-fragranced flowers. I've since added more in various parts of the garden, all in rather wet conditions, and am happy with their highly seasonal interest when in flower. They grow quite slowly the first few years after planting, but make a pleasant tree with a graceful, open manner once established.

Because of the wet conditions, willows have been a mainstay of the garden. I've traditionally used several kinds (*Salix udensis* 'Sekka', *S. alba* var. *vitellina* 'Britzensis', and *S. koriyanagi* 'Rubykins') to create permanent structure, add seasonal interest, and screen the deer-exclusion fence. The willows near the edges of the garden form large, billowy masses that carry the eye upward to the taller trees outside, helping to borrow the outside landscape and make it part of the

garden. Unfortunately, three visually prominent *S. udensis* 'Sekka', which were major features around the stone circle, had to be removed in late summer of 2020 because of insect damage and disease, and I replaced them with *Magnolia virginiana.* If I could have found three other, more massive, densely leaved trees immediately available, I would probably have chosen them, but I had to act quickly if I didn't want to leave such a prominent area bare for many months. The transparent effect given by the magnolias is entirely different from the shade and seclusion created by the willows, but I'm hoping to give this area a new, though different, look—transparent and open, rather than moody and dark. A new Asian pest, the spotted lantern fly (*Lycorma delicatula*), which has no predators on this continent, may be making an end to the use of willows in the garden, certainly some Asian ones. Only time will tell.

I have several viburnum species and all perform quite well. In fact, one, doublefile viburnum (*Viburnum plicatum* f. *tomentosum* 'Mariesii') was original to the woods I cut to the ground before starting the garden. It grew back after about 12 years. I've debated whether to keep it or not, since its heavy, dense foliage lacks

RIGHT Shrubs used as perennials. In many cases, herbaceous perennials in the garden are as large or larger than some shrubs, so I mix them rather indiscriminately when they look appropriate and are able to grow and be managed successfully together, as shown in this view of the lower reflecting pool.

BELOW Mixed hydrangeas, willows, grasses, and background woods seen from the area of the thinking bench.

THE VIEW FROM FEDERAL TWIST

ABOVE A small tree in the prairie: *Cercis canadensis* 'Hearts of Gold'. The color choice is obvious.

the transparency I'd prefer in this location at the center of the garden. On the other hand, its profuse flowers, bright red berries, and colorful autumn foliage are significant desirable characteristics. I compromised this year and cut it back by half. Another *Viburnum plicatum*, which I planted at a corner of the bank overlooking the reflecting pool, is a definite keeper. It anchors that point well and draws the eye to the pool, which isn't otherwise visible from many points in the garden.

Other viburnums that do well are native cultivars *Viburnum nudum* 'Winterthur' and BRANDYWINE with large lustrous leaves that color well in autumn, and berries that turn from pink to dark blue; the native arrowwood *Viburnum dentatum;* and the almost ubiquitous black haw *Viburnum prunifolium*, a small tree endemic to two areas of the garden, with jammy, purple drupes and colorful leaves in autumn. Most of these trees droop from age, giving them a distinctive silhouette.

A small tree I'd like to use more is the vigorously suckering cutleaf smooth sumac (*Rhus glabra* 'Laciniata'). Knowing it detests wet conditions, I looked for a dryish spot and planted it on the bank at one end of the house, where it took off and scrambled up to the gravel terrace. It appears ready to eat the house. I do have to cut out suckers each spring, but I love having a virtual miniature forest on the terrace. The mounding, highly cut foliage is beautiful, especially when it glows bright red in autumn, and the bare twisted stems are like abstract sculpture in winter, especially in fog and snow. At the base of the bank, where the *Rhus glabra* moved up, leaving bare spots, I used miscanthus as cover for a time, but I recently removed this and added several smaller sweet sumacs (*Rhus aromatica*), which should cover the lower bank well and complement the *Rhus glabra* above.

The native sassafras (*Sassafras albidum*) with its mitten-shaped leaves, great autumn color, and wildlife value (it's host to the spicebush swallowtail butterfly) is a very desirable small tree. I like it so much that I've killed several. They simply die in wet conditions, and it has taken several tries for me to finally admit defeat and accept that they do not have the 'ecological amplitude' (James Hitchmough's phrase) to survive in my garden—except on the bank where they come up from seed dropped by birds. Unfortunately, there isn't room for them under the large sycamores, so I coppice them and hope for the best.

Many other small trees and shrubs grow well, as I expected, in wet conditions. Chief among them are the characterful multi-trunked river birches *Betula nigra* HERITAGE; they are fast growers and their decorative peeling park is an eye-catcher even through winter. The native *Aronia arbutifolia* 'Brilliantissima' and *A. melanocarpa*, with red and black berries respectively, make a transparent veil of small flowers on thin, delicate branches in spring; in autumn their small leaves create speckles of red in the landscape. Winterberry hollies (*Ilex verticillata*) produce a profusion of red, and some golden, berries in autumn that look

BELOW A large *Viburnum plicatum* f. *tomentosum* 'Mariesii' (doublefile viburnum) on the bank overlooking the lower reflecting pool in autumn.

THE VIEW FROM FEDERAL TWIST

LEFT AND BELOW Two cultivars of *Ilex verticillita* (winterberry holly), with gold berries (top) and red berries (bottom).

especially appealing against the tawny browns and yellows of dying grasses and perennials.

The native spice bush (*Lindera benzoin*), which is vastly different in appearance from the Asian *Lindera angustifolia*, is a spring wonder in the surrounding forest when thousands of them simultaneously open small flowers that cover the woods like a golden field of tiny yellow stars. They can grow in huge numbers because deer do not eat them. I have a few spice bushes in the garden, but without a large mass of them, their best offering is habitat value and butter yellow leaves in autumn.

Another shrubby visual component of the garden is arborvitae (*Thuja occidentalis*), a native shrub that is widely overused for suburban hedges but is actually a beautiful conical evergreen tree that grows well in wet conditions. I use them as a hedge in one part of the garden and as vertical accents in several places, where they suggest human-like presences.

Among other trees and shrubs are sweetgum (*Liquidambar styraciflua*), Japanese maple (*Acer japonicum*), beauty bush (*Kolkwitzia amabilis* 'Maradco' DREAM CATCHER), *Corylopsis pauciflora*, beauty berry (*Callicarpa dichotoma* 'Issai') and, surprisingly, several boxwoods (*Buxus*). Trees I've recently added to trial are katsura (*Cercidiphyllum japonicum*) and bald cypress (*Taxodium distichum*), which I have no doubt will like the wet conditions.

The surrounding large forest trees are mostly maple (*Acer*) species, oak (*Quercus*)

species, hickory (*Carya*) species, tulip tree (*Liriodendron tulipifera*), white pine (*Pinus strobus*), and red cedar (*Juniperus virginiana*). The forest is full of beech (*Fagus grandifolia*) but, because of forest cutting in the past, it does not yet grow in the garden. When it arrives, if I make the decision to keep it, I'll have to decide whether to start the garden on a transition to a more woodland habitat, because it's such a large, opaque tree.

When I consider the number of trees and shrubs I've listed (and there are more), it would seem there is hardly open space enough for a prairie garden, much less other garden areas. That isn't the case, because I planted many of them along pathways and edges and many are placed to help the garden 'borrow' the landscape outside. When they are in the central part of the garden, I give attention to using 'transparent' foliage and open structure so trees and shrubs blend in naturally with the herbaceous plantings.

CLOCKWISE FROM TOP LEFT
The native *Viburnum prunifolium*,
Magnolia virginiana with cone-like
fruits and red berries, and bright
red fruits of *Viburnum plicatum*
f. *tomentosum* 'Mariesii'.

The seasons

My planting style—using large, highly competitive perennials and grasses—has created an immersive garden of texture, shape, and abundance that changes radically from spring, through summer, into autumn and winter. Abundant growth almost overwhelms the summer garden, then recedes as photosynthesis slows and fails. Textures of plants coarsen with age; then some vanish, and some, like the leaves of *Silphium terebinthinaceum*, develop a magical patina. A few shapes remain stable, many collapse. The garden is like a slow-motion explosion, transient but eternally repetitive. Ironically, this cycle of change is permanence too ... what a joy to watch the show go by, because I watch it, not at a time, but from a place—my garden—where, to quote Tim Richardson, one of the great writers on gardens, I can 'lose the idea of time'.

> Everything we do and perceive has to happen in some place. We cannot imagine time without place, and when we do, we call it limbo or hell. But you can have place without time. I would suggest that a date in the diary is more of a place than a time . . . We tend to think of death as the end of a life lived through time, and imagine that what we fear about death is the sudden extinction of that life. But perhaps this fundamental fear of death is founded not in anticipation of the absence of life, but in a fear of suddenly being nowhere . . . To be in no place, psychologically speaking, is the worst fate of all, since it means either madness or death, whereas to be in a place that is right is paradise—which brings us back to our beloved gardens. . .

> There is a beautiful paradox at the heart of landscapes and gardens. In one sense, gardens are clearly at the mercy of time—in the shape of the seasons and the passage of the day. They change continually. But this enslavement to the movements of the sun and the moon also imbues them with a tangible timelessness. Their very mutability instils in them solidity and inspires reverence. In gardens, we tend to look in on ourselves and lose the idea of time.
> Tim Richardson, 'Psychotopia', in *Vista: The Culture and Politics of Gardens*, 2005

In the changes brought by the passing of the days and the turning of the seasons, one can experience a 'tangible timelessness'. I believe this is much like the 'landscape of the mind' I felt describing those long-ago visits to Rome—place and time condensed, felt in the body, held in the mind, as I saw—and, in the remembering, time is lost and place becomes that prostrate *Cercis siliquastrum* on the Palatine Hill.

SPRING

We always welcome spring by cutting and burning the garden. It happens only once a year, and has become something of a ritual. Depending on the weather, this may be done anytime from mid-January to early March. Because prairie needs to be burned to maintain its health, burning has been a part of the care of the garden from the start. But, having become more aware of the large numbers and species of invertebrate life forms that overwinter in the earth, and in stems of grasses and other plants, I now burn far less. I usually burn grasses individually using a small propane torch. As the dry miscanthus almost explodes, I keep water running nearby and dress appropriately so I can move quickly away from the flame. Milton cuts most of the rest of the garden with a weed strimmer, then removes any debris that isn't burned by hand to the biomass disposal area secreted behind a log wall in an inconspicuous corner of the woodland garden.

BELOW It may not look like spring but it is—after cutting and burning.

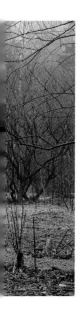

This process usually takes two or three days, and we try to do it when some snow is on the ground to be safe. It's very important not to burn near trees or shrubs, so Milton will move dried grasses and pile them in safe areas for burning.

After the cutting and burning, spring arrives very slowly. The ground is bare for six to eight weeks, and much of it is covered by grass and perennial stubble left so insects can complete their life cycles. I prefer the look of a thorough debris removal and clean burn, but that's not advisable with the precipitous decline in insect populations around the world. Eggs need to hatch, bees need to leave their winter hideaways. Following the fullness of the garden from summer into winter, this lean visual regimen is actually a welcome change. For the first time in a year, I can see all the paths and garden structure at a glance. If I leave a few grasses standing in the mostly empty garden, the lean look can be melancholy and pleasing.

For many years I discouraged visitors in the spring, thinking the garden didn't offer enough interest. I don't say that now. When spring arrives, it quickly pushes up a complex tapestry of low plants in intricate patterns, each fitted to its place over years of living in community. It's an entertaining pastime to look closely as the first layer of plants emerges, knowing this one will grow to only 1ft (30cm) in height, while that one may grow to 7ft (2m). It's also a time to start thinking about the space these plants will occupy as they grow to mature size. It helps to be prepared for necessary adjustments, eliminating some plants, letting others stay.

Later in the season, plants that were a low carpet for the several preceding weeks, responding to ample rain, sun, and the warming earth, begin to swell. The rush to growth is swift and exciting, and at times just a bit frightening. The plants come thick and lush.

Before summer, the early spring carpet is well along the way to maturity, making the actual transition to summer somewhat irrelevant. The plants simply grow larger, so the look of the garden doesn't substantially change until well into high summer.

OPPOSITE AND THIS PAGE Burning on the bank is no longer possible (top left) because it would kill nearby shrubs, so we cut the grasses on the bank (bottom left), remove a portion, and burn in a safer location, but only when necessary. Much of the garden is simply cut with a strimmer (above), left long to allow overwintering insects to complete their life cycles, then cut more finely later. After the cleanup (center), a few grasses are left standing for a while to create a park-like atmosphere.

THIS PAGE Spring carpet, clockwise from top: an emerging mix, some by random seeding, of *Alchemilla mollis* (never self-seeds in my garden), *Onoclea sensibilis*, *Silphium perfoliatum*, *Eupatorium perfoliatum*, equisetum; a large colony of *Onoclea sensibilis*; a varied carpet of grasses and perennials around the circle of red logs; and another view of *Onoclea sensibilis* with equisetum and *Silphium perfoliatum* just emerging.

LEFT Spring carpet: *Petasites hybridus* × Dutch in flower with equisetum and one highly dissected leaf of *Ligularia japonica* (top), a mass of *Onoclea sensibilis* with equisetum, *Hemerocallis fulva*, and several silphium behind (middle), and *Packera aurea* in flower with sanguisorba rising from it (bottom).

LEFT *Ligularia japonica* in flower against a sea of petasites.

BELOW RIGHT Several plants that will become tall emergents—*Silphium laciniatum*, *Silphium perfoliatum*, *Inula racemosa* 'Sonnenspeer'—among other, much shorter plants: equisetum, sanguisorba, *Euphorbia palustris*, and solidago.

BOTTOM RIGHT *Maianthemum racemosum* (false Solomon's seal) rising through a carpet of equisetum.

CLOCKWISE FROM TOP
Maianthemum racemosum
(again) about to flower;
Dryopteris erythrosora; the
bare garden revealing major
pathways after the annual
cutting and burning in very
early spring; the golden
umbelliferous flower of
Euphorbia palustris.

CLOCKWISE FROM TOP *Hosta sieboldiana*, which surprisingly self-seeds in the dry gravel under a *Platanus occidentalis* (sycamore); a flowering *Cephalanthus occidentalis* (button bush); the canal pond in late afternoon light surrounded by new growth of water-loving perennials and grasses; and *Iris virginica* 'Contraband Girl'.

ABOVE From the mud garden, a view of the rapidly rising prairie struck by beams of sunlight filtering through the trees, one of many examples of the chiaroscuro effects in the garden.

RIGHT More chiaroscuro lighting from the late afternoon sun.

THIS PAGE Spring light three ways: a partly cloudy sky emphasizes the highly suggestive, rising towers of *Silphium perfoliatum* below the house (top); bright sunlight casts deep shadows, giving the same silphium sharply defined forms, a kind of knife-edge sharpness that suggests threat (middle); a cloudy day washes away detail, leaving only broad masses of green (bottom).

PLANTING THE GARDEN

RIGHT Sharp contrast of brightness and deep shadow is the nature of a clearing in the woods. Here, the prairie, brightly lit, against the dark background of woods.

SUMMER

In the early years, the prairie garden was quite grassy and open. I liked the effect, but it was transient. The photograph opposite of my friend Ernst with his camera was taken early in the summer of 2009. This is a pleasant light meadow effect, but the garden was too open, too much earth was exposed, and without a stabilizing matrix, rapid change was inevitable. This photograph always reminds me of the many choices I made, and other choices I might have made to keep this appearance.

In spring the garden space is like a bowl of irregular shape, with walls of forest trees surrounding a relatively flat bottom. As plants grow, that flat bottom becomes articulated in innumerable ways; the plants rise to varying heights and densities and many grow above your head. 'Immersive' is the word to describe it. What was a flat plain becomes a second, elevated landscape. In spring you look down to the garden; in summer, you look up.

Midsummer is the peak season for the flowery prairie plants. First *Filipendula ulmaria*, then the long drift of *Filipendula rubra* 'Venusta' flowering in shocking pink (I much prefer it after the flowers fade to a rich bronze color). Next the *Silphium perfoliatum*, with *S. laciniatum* following close on, then the graceful, tall, elegant wands of *S. terebinthinaceum* come into flower. Next the *Eupatorium* (*maculatum*, *purpureum*, various kinds, even a very tall clump from a woodland edge in North Carolina), which are very late risers, come into bloom. All these plants have good, strong structure, but our violent thunderstorms push them into leaning towers and banks of flowery allure—and for a while the garden dances with color and throws yellow daisies against the sky.

A note on yellow. There was a time when I said yellow wasn't allowed in my garden, but as I long ago accepted the ecology here as a given, I had to accept the plants that could live here. Many of them are prairie plants, and many of those

BELOW Ernst, taking a photograph, in the much more loosely, and more sparsely planted, summer prairie of the past. I sometimes think I might want to return the garden to this earlier, looser phase, but always decide to let it continue along the path it has taken.

PLANTING THE GARDEN

RIGHT Making a wide arc in late summer, the sun comes around behind the house and lights the prairie from behind. Tall *Inula racemosa* 'Sonnenspeer' flowering at right, and *Molinia caerulea* subsp. *arundinacea* 'Skyracer' at left.

CLOCKWISE FROM TOP LEFT
Sanguisorba officinalis 'Pink
Tanna'; deeply cut, hairy foliage of
Silphium laciniatum; *Sanguisorba
tenuifolia* 'Purpurea'; *Pycnanthe-
mum muticum* (mountain mint);
Hydrangea paniculata with
a yellow swallowtail butterfly.

that thrive in this ecology have yellow flowers. So my initial 'acceptance of what was given' still applies, even to yellow. I do still look for other colors, but there are few for this environment. One is a monkshood (*Aconitum carmichaelii*); its extremely late dark blue is an extraordinary contrast against the colors of autumn, but it will grow only on the bank. The garden is too wet. Another is native to the site—great blue lobelia (*Lobelia siphilitica*), and it does tolerate wet well. I do add seed to increase the late blue.

Some see the large, lush foliage, huge plants, and think: 'primordial'. I admit the garden can have a jungly, tropical look at times, a bit of an Henri Rousseau quality, but that's a passing fantasy. It's certainly not my intent, but others see it, so it must be so.

From late July into August the prairie becomes a dense mixture of bumps, humps, and leaning verticals, full of detail emerging at various levels. The prairie is the only part of the garden you can't enter, except for one cross path that feels like a tunnel in this late season. Most of the garden is 'permeable'; you can work your way through almost anywhere. Only in the prairie are you locked out, yet another example of the garden gently pushing back. You must think how to deal with it. (Not a difficult problem; you can simply walk around it, looking in.)

With the passing of the summer equinox, the angle of the sun drops lower and as the days go by, morning shadows of the tall trees stretch across the garden, making the whole of it a mass of moving shadow and light. The colors of green and the light effects are myriad but peaceful. When I rise, I usually spend the morning hours where I can look out at this canvas of modulating greens. The sunlight reflects off the miscanthus leaves like silver while beside it the broader leaves of aralia filter a soft light through them. The sun's rays are modulated, constantly changing, as if a sea surface were refracting light through moving waves stirred by the breeze.

As the heat of August becomes more intense, flowering decreases and portents of autumn become visible. As I look out on hot, bright mornings, the relentless brilliant sunlight limns the outlines and edges of green shapes with a golden aura while everything else is cast into shadow. This is an intense contrast, agreeable to see, particularly from a distance, breaking up the field of vision in a sort of pointillist way and suggesting flat pattern rather than depth and three-dimensional form. The flat, pattern-like appearance suggests other forms of art, like a painting or a patterned fabric.

This is a phenomenon of the morning, however, when the sun is slightly behind the wall of trees, then directly overhead. As it progresses westward, the sense of three-dimensionality returns as shafts of light and dark spread across the landscape, erasing the flat patterning of the morning.

As the sun becomes lower in the sky through September and temperatures drop, the plant foliage will reach its allotted age and begin failing, and the forest behind the garden will let in more light. The autumnal equinox is near, but the colors of autumn usually hold off until mid- to late October.

TOP ROW Looking up the bank from canal pond to house (left) and woodland garden at midday (right).

CENTRE ROW *Eupatorium maculatum* (Joe Pye weed); *Filipendula rubra* 'Venusta' flower in bud; *Rumex hydrolapathum* (tall, glaucous, narrow leaves) by canal pond; *Eryngium yuccifolium* (rattlesnake master).

BOTTOM ROW *Asclepias tuberosa* (milkweed) in flower behind *Chasmanthium latifolium* on the terrace; Wave Hill chairs vanishing in increasingly tall growth on the immersion path.

AUTUMN

One year heavy rains may come day after day from high summer and into autumn; in others, drought withers the plants. But always a certain degree of random abstraction transforms plant groupings. Chance combinations of shapes, diagonal and vertical lines, textures, and colors make designs that suggest abstract paintings, or perhaps Rorschach inkblots. In late autumn especially, I see scenes that look like Expressionist paintings. Gears shift, chemistry changes as temperatures drop, chlorophyll dies, revealing the underlying colors. The transformation to autumn becomes visible.

As the silphium disintegrate, the inula finish their flowers and, as they age, begin to slowly build character, turning from green to brown, finally to a leaden gray to black when wet in late autumn, and their leaves droop from upright arched curves to limp verticals that look as if they had melted. The garden darkens. The giant ironweeds (*Vernonia* spp.) show their tall, dark purple colors, the New

BELOW In October morning light, *Viburnum plicatum* f. *tomentosum* 'Mariesii' (doublefile viburnum) overlooking the lower reflecting pool. The coloring varies, but this year it was an especially bright red. *Miscanthus* behind, *Spartina pectinata* (prairie cordgrass) in foreground.

CLOCKWISE FROM TOP LEFT
Looking up to the house with
its unusual 'swooping' chimney
ornament, through autumn
foliage of *Viburnum nudum*
'Winterthur' and *Aster tartaricus*;
fruit of an unidentified legacy crab
apple planted when the
house was built in 1965; dark
purple flower of *Aconitum
carmichaelii* with colorful autumn
foliage of various shrubs on
the bank; seed heads of vernonia;
Wave Hill chairs veiled by the
darkening foliage around the
immersion path.

RIGHT *Rhus glabra* 'Laciniata' in fiery red on the terrace (top); from left to right near the house entrance, *Lindera angustifolia*, still green *Parrotia persica*, red *Euonymous alatus*, another very tall *Lindera angustifolia*, and two spires of *Thuja occidentalis* pruned as pointy lollipops (middle); *Rhus glabra*, dark spires of inula, and miscanthus flowering on the terrace (bottom).

LEFT A foreshortened view from the terrace across to a bench on a main path, with a pollarded *Salix alba* var. *vitellina* 'Britzensis' near the center (top); *Symphyotrichum lateriflorum*, one of the asters growing wild in the garden (middle); the passage from the woodland garden into the prairie as leaves are falling from the trees (bottom).

CLOCKWISE FROM TOP LEFT
Autumnal drama: sculptural leaves of *Inula racemosa*; sun breaking into the shadowy darkness of *Hydrangea paniculata* in the thinking bench corner; *Asclepias tuberosa* releasing its seed to the wind; the tall multi-stem snag in the light of the rising sun; Wave Hill chairs in fading foliage along the immersion path.

England asters (*Symphyotricum novae-angliae*) finish their violets, purples, and pinks, and the sanguisorbas hang on, flopping and drooping one way and another. The last are the white *Sanguisorba canadensis*, which seem to flower for months, some retaining an unexpected, graceful, and tenuous verticality.

Autumn, I think, is the time when the truest nature of the garden comes to the fore. As plants lose their green energy and the life processes slow and begin to fail, the garden takes on warm brown, red, yellow, and glowing orange shades that evoke seemingly contradictory moods of melancholy and plenitude. Rough, damaged, imperfect, the late autumn plants exhibit amazing character.

As the season advances, decaying organic matter begins a slow process of decomposition, and sweet smells of fermentation perfume the air. The biological processes in the woodland environment are not unlike cider-making, the rising of sourdough bread, fermenting grape must. As you walk, sweet, musty odors rise from the ferment below.

The mood, the *Stimmung*, of the garden changes rather theatrically as the green of summer transforms into a dramatic backdrop of, first, picturesque autumn scenes, then of rain, fog, and ice, a continually changing moody landscape. If it were possible for a garden to think, it would be thinking its deepest thoughts.

BELOW Weather, clouds, the quality of the light are all part of the landscape garden.

THE VIEW FROM FEDERAL TWIST

LEFT The origin of the landscape garden is in painting … with Claude Lorraine and others who wanted to awaken thoughts of the classical world … and for Americans, the Picturesque paintings of the Hudson River School, where we often see a preference for darkness, pensive thoughtfulness, and melancholy. To me, this is the landscape garden at its best.

RIGHT Finding beauty in collapse and decay: a field of grasses crushed by an early snow (top); inulas standing like dark, spectral sculptures on a dreary late autumn day (middle); glowing grasses contrast with the dark, foggy woods (bottom).

LEFT Finding beauty in collapse and decay: the big inulas have a presence, not unlike human figures, and might appear to be walking among the grasses (top); dying hydrangea blossoms appear to block the way (middle); a whisp of memory is stirred by dark seed heads and stems against the cream-colored grasses (bottom).

RIGHT An early autumn sunrise from the terrace.

THE VIEW FROM FEDERAL TWIST

CLOCKWISE FROM TOP Finding beauty in collapse and decay: fading flowers of *Patrinia scabiosifolia*, inula and grasses block the view of the garden below and make these terrace plantings appear to be a part of the more distant woods (fog helps); seed pods of *Apocynum cannibinum*; the highly photogenic structures that hold the seed of *Ligularia japonica*, after the seeds have fallen or blown away; peeling bark of *Acer griseum* (paperbark maple).

LEFT Finding beauty in collapse and decay: as the mass of foliage falls away, and with fog, this perhaps could be a scene from a German film set in the Middle Ages (top); *Pennisetum alopecuroides* 'Moudry' surrounds a ceramic urn (middle); grasses tumbling down the bank from the terrace to the area of the lower reflecting pool (bottom).

THE VIEW FROM FEDERAL TWIST

WINTER

Winter seems to be either very dramatic or boring. A good rain can make the dull grasses luminous, almost as if they were radiating light from within. Fog adds mystery to any landscape, and snow and ice can make the garden a magical cliché.

Our winters are unpredictable. I remember one heavy wet snow on the last day of October reduced the garden to ruins, but this is extraordinarily early for so much snow. In other winters, we may have no snow cover at all, only a few snow showers. We rarely have days with photogenic hoarfrost. Icy rains and nor'easters with driving, heavy snow are more usual—but the result can be beautiful.

I tend to turn inward during winter, indulging in the pleasures of the mental landscape, reading, and walking in the garden on more pleasant days, keeping watch for structural failures and collapses. And after the turn of the year, since our winter weather is so inconsistent and unpredictable, I try to project when I'll

BELOW After a storm, the morning sun is eclipsed by a *Platanus occidentalis* (sycamore) encased in a skin of ice.

　　THE VIEW FROM FEDERAL TWIST

LEFT How winter changes things: a light snow isolates the house above the garden (top); black inula spires catch cups of snow (middle); *Typha latifolia* (cattail) lends a bit of color to the whitened landscape (bottom).

need to call Milton to schedule the days for cutting and burning.

I will continue to allow chance to have a say, experiment not on the plants but with the plant communities, and continue to live intensely with the garden. And late every winter, I will wipe the garden away, burning what I can and cutting down the rest in preparation for whatever next year brings.

Thinking back to the original wild landscape, I remind myself that constraints presented opportunities, opening a door to a new kind of gardening I would never have envisioned had I been offered a more compliant site.

RIGHT Twig detail (above); winter scene from the terrace (below).

LEFT A very different winter view towards the house (top); stone circle in snow (middle); the multi-stem snag in snow (bottom).

RIGHT Winter abstract.

ARRIVAL AT FEDERAL TWIST

The most meaningful measure
of a garden's success is its
power to steer emotions and
ignite the imagination.

Michael Van Valkenburgh, *Designing a Garden*

THE VIEW FROM FEDERAL TWIST

So I'm telling you about the entrance at the end of the book. Perhaps an explanation is in order?

I've done things backwards more than once in making this garden. I use the Michael Van Valkenburgh quotation opposite to clarify my priorities. At the start, I was preoccupied with the main garden—concerned far more with how to 'steer emotions' and 'ignite the imagination' than with a formal approach to garden design. Simply put, the garden itself was the point, and I wasn't particularly interested in how you get into it.

So my approach to the entrance garden was minimal and a bit hit or miss. Though I treated it as entirely separate from the main garden, it's turned out to be more than satisfactory, in many ways. Actually, it has become a unity with the rest of the garden, as you'll see.

Fitting the pieces together

I've waited so long to mention the arrival area, I should show you how all the pieces fit together—entrance garden, main garden, woodland, house, terrace. In the aerial photograph of the house, the garden, and the surrounding landscape, the entrance garden is at the top, adjacent to the gravel parking area and the house; the much larger main garden is at the bottom, on the opposite side of the house, and the terrace runs across the length of the house, an approximately 20-ft-deep (6-m-deep) ledge about 12ft (3.6m) above the main garden (and mostly hidden by the canopy of golden-leaved sycamores that shade much of the house). Between them is a rather steep bank dropping down to the lower garden. In this view you can see that the garden is physically unified; it wraps around the house.

OPPOSITE Garden and entrance garden are one. The garden surrounds the house.

The arrival sequence isn't intended to impress—simply to set a mood and tone for the garden, and to serve as a sign. The house is well back from the road, rather distant and lonely amid the trees, making it seem like a part of the forest. If nothing else, you certainly know by the character of this setting that you're not about to visit a rose garden.

The entrance garden is immediately adjacent to the front porch of the house. From the drive it looks like a great green blur. It obscures most of the house, adding to the impression the house is emerging from forest. Only recently, I've begun to use wood from ash trees lost to a catastrophic ash dieback to create a forest floor ecology between the road and the house.

Like the rest of the garden, this is a novel ecology. I'm placing logs and branches on the earth, allowing them to decay naturally, as a kind of experiment in *Hugelkultur* (a German term meaning mound or hill culture) with which I hope to improve the soil in spots in order to grow shade plants not suited to the existing heavy clay soil. It is also a beneficial use of waste wood. Around the wood, I'm planting masses of ferns, carex, grasses, ligularia, and spring ephemerals, which I know from experience the deer will not eat, as well as a highly resilient Asian shrub, *Lindera angustifolia*, and the native spicebush (*Lindera benzoin*), which are also not browsed by deer. The lindera will eventually create an understory of shrubs and small trees to complement the existing, large, and very old *Viburnum*

prunifolium that have always grown in this area. This is a long-term experiment and I don't expect it to have power to 'ignite the imagination', as Michael Van Valkenburgh puts it, for several years.

The space nearest the house is much further along. This was originally a rough graveled circle of decaying trees—remnants of what had once been an entrance garden—a curving pathway from the parking area to the front door, with two rotting Japanese cherry trees, an anonymous stick tree in its center, some scraggly stems of burning bush (*Euonymus alatus*) and four small arborvitae (*Thuja occidentalis*) on the side toward the garage. It was barren and ugly. I removed the Japanese cherries, which were extraordinarily out of place in this wooded American site, and almost all the other living things. I left two of the four *Thuja occidentalis* temporarily (so I thought). I had brought some *Erianthus ravennae* from our former house, and I placed these at the front corner of the rough gravel circle. I knew the grass would eventually grow to about 12 ft (3.6m) tall, so it would make a major statement.

Across the entrance walk from the erianthus was a hedge of burning bush. On the opposite side of the hedge, I built a low stone circle to subtly reflect the existing gravel circle, adding a little spatial continuity to the front garden. I planted *Miscanthus sinensis* 'Adagio' around much of the inner circumference with the intention of creating a deer deterrent. (None of the entrance garden has deer exclusion fencing.) I have to admit I haven't found many plants that will grow in this area and resist deer predation. Fortunately, the grasses, bracken, and some self-seeded inula and ligularia are visually acceptable until I find a more permanent, aesthetically acceptable solution. I still experiment with plants, even at the entrance to my garden.

At one side of the circle, three low steps lead to a gravel path that curves around the end of the house to the main garden on the opposite side. A legacy planting of very tall burning bush along that length of the house was the only living thing there, and I decided to keep it; the ground level drops off, and the rough hedge of euonymus screens the bare concrete foundation.

As a trial, I bought three or four *Ligularia dentata* 'Desdemona' and 'Othello' at the Union Square Green Market near my office in Manhattan, where quite a few of my trial plants were acquired, and placed them in front of the euonymus. To my surprise, these few plants self-seeded with abandon. They have now become a featured ground cover and they flower across the full length of the house. They do a magnificent job of covering the ground where needed, even behaving well when they insert themselves among grasses and other perennials, and they are totally deer-proof. Most notable for me, however, is their large leathery foliage, which I like, and evocative stems and seed heads in autumn. Though the foliage does wilt in hot sun, it always perks up later. Across the path from the euonymus wall,

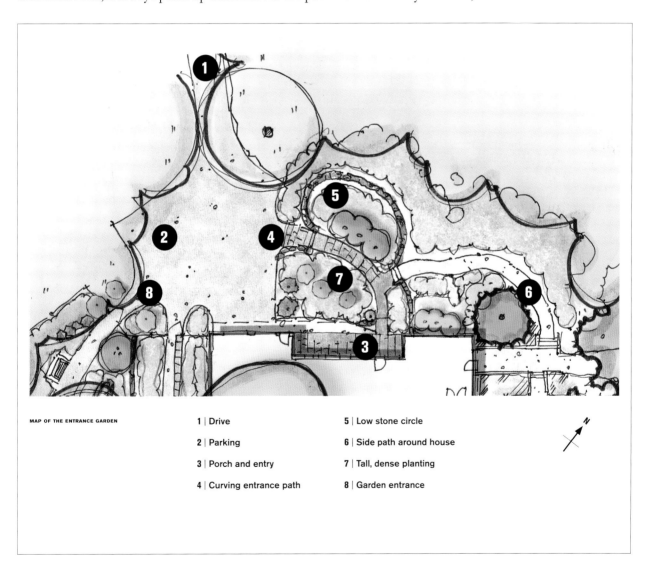

MAP OF THE ENTRANCE GARDEN

1 | Drive

2 | Parking

3 | Porch and entry

4 | Curving entrance path

5 | Low stone circle

6 | Side path around house

7 | Tall, dense planting

8 | Garden entrance

I planted a variety of *Miscanthus* cultivars to add a grassy look and as a further deer deterrent, since deer dislike grasses.

I've given the impression that Federal Twist is a garden hidden behind the wall of the house, and much of it is, though I didn't set out to make a hidden garden. I can't say I gave much thought to it; this is simply the nature of the place. It's also a result of having to fence in the garden to keep deer out. Now I realize the idea of a hidden garden is important to how you experience Federal Twist. I accept this, though with a reluctance I find hard to explain. (While the concept of 'hidden' is relevant, 'behind' is misleading. That's just a convenience of speech. I was raised in America, where almost everyone has a 'front yard' and a 'back yard' and it's hard to break that front-back habit of thinking, even when there is no front or back. If you just make everything garden, you don't have to worry about such things.)

As is typical of many mid-1960s houses, ours has two main linear façades—a plain one facing the public road and a more articulated façade facing the main garden and the woods. The entrance garden, though it extends in a linear fashion across the façade of the house, expands at the center of the facade, into a tall, blousy, dense circle of vegetation like some strange baroque ornament. Taken altogether, however, the entrance garden is far easier to grasp at a glance—because it's a far simpler layout—than the main garden, which is complex, extensive, and blends into the surrounding woods.

There's not a lot of room in this center area, but I wanted to make a big effect using height, shape, texture, and color. This little garden takes its form predominantly from vertical elements and mounding shapes. By autumn it resembles something like a fireworks display. Two large *Thuja occidentalis* on the right are the most visually dominant vertical elements (these are the two of four I left in place years before, intending to remove them). These are highly prone to deer browsing, so the trunks are bare up to a height of about 5ft (1.5m). A number of people have

THE VIEW FROM FEDERAL TWIST

told me they think these look odd. I find the quirky shape delightful, and it saves this common, overused tree from banality. And because they are evergreen, they give the entrance to the house a clearly identifiable look even in winter.

At the curving entrance walk around to the front door are the now large *Erianthus ravennae*, one of the largest grasses that grows in our area and a rather flamboyant one. Its autumn plumes add a celebratory feeling, and as the tall flowering stalks age, they turn a pleasing reddish-purple. Across the walk is a *Parrotia persica* and behind it is the hedge of burning bush. At a 90-degree angle behind it is a row of three *Lindera angustifolia*, all adjacent to the secondary stone circle.

After all these years, I'm still not certain about my priorities in making this garden, but chief among them were privacy and delight, especially from inside the house. And, of course, I wanted the entry garden to be a sign, like a beacon, to let you know you've arrived (the tall erianthus and thuja certainly do that). I also wanted it to be a bit of a shock, to shake up expectations and to clearly mark this as a transitional space where you start the process of 'feeling' your way into the garden. I'd like to think of it as a transformational place, but perhaps I wish for too much.

The center cluster of plants is a barrier that blocks a free view of the door. Visitors not familiar with the entrance usually pause, a little mystified, because they have to move around the plants to find the door, an act some people may feel is transgressive. I could say this was not my intention, but I'm not so sure that's true. I do want the entrance to signal solitude, mystery, seclusion, privacy—not to be unwelcoming, but to disrupt any feelings of complacency. A moment of uncertainty as to how to make contact can feel like being momentarily lost, then finding the way. This loosening of the emotions can make room for other things to happen, and can prepare for the transition into the main garden. Nevertheless, when new visitors arrive, I nearly always obey an impulse to go out the front door, greet them, and guide them in.

On the next page is a view of the planted circle from the front door. Moving roughly clockwise from the lower left is *Hakonechloa macra* 'Aureola' with *Helleborus foetidus* beside it; *Ligularia dentata* running along to the far end; a *Cotinus coggygria* 'Grace' midway; one of two bare-trunked *Thuja occidentalis* at the end; some *Inula racemosa* 'Sonnenspeer' just becoming visible; a large swathe of *Eupatorium maculatum* hiding the *Erianthus*, which is still very low; a *Lindera angustifolia* var. *glabra*; more *Eupatorium*; *Panicum virgatum* 'Cloud Nine'; *Cotinus coggygria* 'Velvet Cloak'; *Miscanthus sinensis* 'Adagio'; and in the corner a boxwood. Along the walk are *Patrinia scabiosifolia*, a beauty berry (*Callicarpa dichotoma* 'Issai'), more *Ligularia dentata*, and catmint (*Nepeta* 'Walker's Low'*)*. The shrub across the entrance path is golden beauty bush (*Kolkwitzia amabilis* 'Maradco' DREAM CATCHER), and the tall hedge at top right is burning bush. The gravel drive up to Federal Twist Road is already hidden behind this relatively low growth.

A note on the burning bush. In the USA, this is considered to be a terribly invasive species that displaces native plants, but in Europe, it's used with no such concern. I feel some American readers will excoriate me for keeping it, so I need to address the issue of so-called 'invasive aliens'. It was already present when we bought the house. I looked in the woods around us and found it, as well as *Berberis*

BELOW The view across the entry circle from the house in early summer.

THE VIEW FROM FEDERAL TWIST

LEFT The planting of the entry circle depends on line, form and texture far more than color. Some flowers add color in high summer, but the most colorful aspect of this planting comes in autumn.

thunbergii (Japanese barberry), scattered throughout. I do not believe it will ever be eradicated from our natural areas, and there are other invasive species in my area, such as the common Japanese honeysuckle (*Lonicera japonica*), Russian olive (*Elaeagnus angustifolia*), Japanese wisteria (*Wisteria floribunda*), and others that are far worse offenders. I have to pick my battles, so I focus on removing the really destructive vines and trees I've mentioned and decided to keep the burning bush.

The entry point into the garden is off to the side, across the parking area. Two columns of tall *Miscanthus giganteus* stand on either side of the simple, unassuming gate. The miscanthus, and lower *Panicum virgatum* 'Shenandoah' in front, are disliked by deer, as are the ligularia, so they don't encourage the animals to enter the garden should the gate be left open by accident. However, I use the tall grasses for reasons other than utility. By obscuring the entry, particularly in this autumn view, they add a bit of mystery.

Only years after making this entry did I recognize a similarity to Rousham, where you enter the park through a mysterious, dark hole in the shrubbery.

Randomness and chance

Back in 2005, while talking to the contractor I'd hired to cut down masses of junipers, he remarked that he had been driving by our house for the past 20 years and had never once noticed a dwelling here. The house is wooden, stained the color of bark, so it fades into the background, but when I heard this, I felt almost as if I'd been given a gift—a secret, hidden place. His chance remark has resonated over the years; I recall it again and again as I try to understand this landscape where we now live and its meaning to me.

The idea of a secret garden has become a powerful metaphor. I did not intend to make Federal Twist a secret garden; its physical screening by the bulk of the house, its location on the lower part of a slope, and the fencing needed to keep deer out have made it seem to be, so I suppose it is. It's as if the requisites of the landscape took charge and did what needed to be done.

I should add that—in the course of making the garden—I've several times taken chance remarks and accidents as messages from somewhere 'other'. The tree-feller's off-the-cuff comment, for example, sounded the tone of solitude and privacy I was seeking, whether consciously or not, and acted as a catalyst, starting a series of thoughts about the landscape—so, as one example, I've kept the roadside rough, coarse, and pretty much indistinguishable from the surrounding country roadsides. The entrance to the house can be hard to find.

Randomness and chance happenings, like chance remarks, seem to offer gifts, if only I can decipher them. I don't mean this is magic; it's simply a process of self-exploration and discovery—finding meaning. It's as if randomness roughens up the smooth texture of quotidian reality and makes me see things in a new way. A great part of the mystery of gardening comes, I believe, from such 'accidents'—a word, a sound, an irritation, a minor incident that changes a direction, or introduces new possibilities, new opportunities, a new way of thinking. It's as if the spirit of the place has spoken.

ABOVE Another aspect of the entry circle, looking toward the far end of the house and the woodland garden beyond (top), and the rustic entry gate to the garden partly obscured by a mass of declining brown *Miscanthus giganteus* (bottom).

RETHINKING WHAT A GARDEN CAN BE AND DO

Even after over 50 years of
gardening and visiting gardens,
it made me rethink what a garden
can be and do.

Monty Don, on Federal Twist in *American Gardens* BBC TV series

The constraints of the place where I chose to make a garden were bewildering, and, yes, they were thought-provoking. I set out on a journey, and I had no idea where it would take me. Was it a process of 'rethinking'? Well, certainly 'thinking'— also reading, learning, observing, living in the place as it became a garden.

Before I could even conceive of making a garden in this place, I had to explore many possibilities. Most were out of the ordinary. Some were radical—first, the decision even to try to make a garden on such a difficult site, to accept heavy wet clay soil and not try to improve it, to plant directly into existing vegetation with virtually no site preparation, to avoid tilling or disturbing the land surface and maintaining weeds as cover until I could plant something more to my liking and, finally, to make a landscape garden, which usually connotes immensity, in quite a limited space, a clearing in the woods.

I explored new ideas, I read widely in garden design, landscape architecture, ecology, garden history, the philosophy of gardens, phenomenology, and aesthetics. And probably more important than anything else was this: I explored my feelings about the garden, about my life—I suppose, about everything. I frequently wrote in my blog posts, sometimes quite intimately, about making the garden and the decisions facing me, slowly developing my thoughts about what a garden could be and sharing those ideas.

PREVIOUS PAGES This isn't a typical garden image. I chose it because it suggests another way to look at gardens. Is this space, is this landscape, is this weather, is this emotion? Where in this place do I belong?

OPPOSITE AND BELOW In contrast to that dark landscape on the previous page, the weather, from inside, is sunny; I know I belong here—in that big green chair. Inside, space is constrained, formalized, and sized for human use; light is modulated by the time of day, morning (left) and afternoon (right). This is my 'brown study'.

View from Federal Twist
We Garden in Darkness
April 30, 2012

My life is so arranged (rather, I have so arranged it) that I find myself making frequent late night drives between the city and the country house. I did that last night, after seeing an exceptional play.

On the drive out I felt very much alone, intensely alone, driving through the late darkness, capsuled in my car. Not a loneliness of longing or depression or sadness, but an existential aloneness, a freedom, an epiphany of sorts, recognition that I've been given a gift, the ability to be aware how tiny and insignificant and brief my life is in this dark, measureless, incomprehensible universe.

I understood that everything, my being, my life, all I do comes out of this darkness. Some of us make gardens out of darkness.

* * *

As I sit here today, looking over the green garden, I understand that light is darkness and darkness is light, that I am seeing darkness, that my eyes and brain only interpret various frequencies of electromagnetic radiation as light, color, shape, my two eyes and brain allow me to think I can judge distance and spatial relationships, sensory cells create the illusion of fragrance and touch, ears sound.

And still I know—beneath this all is the cold, unknowable darkness that makes it possible to garden with light.

I took making a garden extremely seriously, almost as if it were a life or death proposition. Perhaps this was owing to my increasing awareness of mortality. My mother and my only sister died during the making of the garden, leaving me alone, the last of my line, and I was nearing retirement age even as I started the garden. So garden-making, though a source of happiness, excitement, and great joy, was always touched with melancholy—by which I do not intend any negative meaning whatsoever. Melancholy is a rich and complex emotion.

What is the garden for?

Each morning, I start my day sitting in my big green chair, with a cup of coffee, looking across the living room out to the garden. It's September now. The bushy grasses glitter like jewels just 20ft (6m) out at the terrace edge, the reflective cuticle of miscanthus foliage shattering sunlight like a broken mirror. Looking farther out, I see the distant line of tall trees—dark-faced woods, shafts of light streaming down among dusky trunks from above.

OVERLEAF The terrace on an autumn day.

This is one of the most important things the garden is for.

Here is another, a comment from a close friend: 'The stone circle surrounded by the multi-stem salix at Federal Twist has always been a favorite spot of mine. It is a place that naturally makes me stop and slow down, listen to nature, feel completely surrounded by plants and, ultimately, it lets my imagination and thoughts take me far away. Well, maybe that's what gardens are for, at least I like to think so' (Giacomo Guzzon, on a visit to Federal Twist, November 2019).

And another: it's a 'garden that works with what the local ecology can support instead of fighting against it. Today was proof that you can do crazy beautiful things with clay and poor draining soils' (A perceptive neighbor, Lin Pérez, on her first visit, late October 2019).

And one more, mine, a kind of participatory drill: turn the page to see the gravel terrace in autumn. Four Adirondack chairs wait empty—anticipating an arrival? . . . Or has someone just departed?

You are alone. No one else is in the house or the garden. What are your feelings as you stand here?

* * *

Perhaps we need to think less about what a garden can be and more about what it can do. Certainly, we need refuge and places of respite, places for laughter and enjoyment, places for pleasure . . . but can we ask for something more than a passive field of restoration? Can the garden 'do' something to change us?

I sit in my green chair, thinking such a thing is possible. You walk in the garden, you see the dying fall of autumn, desiccation, dissolution, you find the path you're on won't get you where you want to be—feeling slightly annoyed, you give up your goal and just listen; perhaps you see something you didn't notice before. You learn to let the garden be the protagonist. This is humility, allowing the 'other' to take precedence, perhaps seeing the garden as a symbol of something larger and much more important.

REFERENCES AND BIBLIOGRAPHY

Bachelard, Gaston. *The Poetics of Space*. New York: Penguin Books. 2014.

Benedito, Silvia. *Atmosphere Anatomies: On Design, Weather, and Sensation*. Zurich: Lars Müller Publishers. 2021.

Bowring, Jacky. *Melancholy and the Landscape: Locating Sadness, Memory and Reflection in the Landscape*. London and New York: Routledge. 2017.

Cooper, David E. *A Philosophy of Gardens*. New York: Oxford University Press. 2006.

Darke, Rick. *The American Woodland Garden: Capturing the Spirit of the Deciduous Forest*. Portland, Oregon: Timber Press. 2002.

Darke, Rick. *The Encyclopedia of Grasses for Livable Landscapes*. Portland, Oregon: Timber Press. 2007.

Don, Monty. *American Gardens* (BBC TV Series). 2020.

Gerritsen, Henk and Piet Oudolf. *Dream Plants for the Natural Garden*. Portland, Oregon: Timber Press. 2000.

Gerritsen, Henk. *Essay on Gardening*. Amsterdam: Architectura & Natura Press. 2008.

Gumbrecht, Hans Ulrich. *Atmosphere, Mood, Stimmung: on a Hidden Potential of Literature*. Stanford University Press. Kindle Edition. 2012.

Hansen, Richard and Friedrich Stahl. *Perennials and their Garden Habitats*. Portland, Oregon: Timber Press. 1993.

Harrison, Robert Pogue. *Gardens: an Essay on the Human Condition*. Chicago: The University of Chicago Press. 2008.

Hitchmough, James. *Sowing Beauty: Designing Flowering Meadows from Seed*. Portland, Oregon: Timber Press. 2017.

Murakami, Haruki. *1Q84*. New York: Alfred A. Knopf. 2011.

Hunt, John Dixon. *A World of Gardens*. London: Reaktion Books. 2012.

King, Michael. *Perennial Garden Design*. Portland, Oregon: Timber Press. 2006.

Kingsbury, Nöel. *Natural Garden Style*. London: Merrell. 2009.

Kingsbury, Nöel. *Planting: A New Perspective*. Portland, Oregon: Timber Press. 2013.

Kingsbury, Nöel. *The New Perennial Garden*. London: Frances Lincoln Limited. 1996.

Kingsbury, Nöel and Piet Oudolf. *Oudolf Hummelo: A Journey through a Plantsman's Life*. New York: The Monacelli Press. 2015.

Madson, John. *Where the Sky Began: Land of the Tallgrass Prairie*. University of Iowa Press. 2004.

Nassauer, Joan Iverson, 1995. 'Messy ecosystems, orderly frames.' *Landscape Journal* 14, no. 2:167-170.

Oudolf, Piet and Rick Darke. *Gardens of the Highline: Elevating the Nature of Modern Landscapes*. Portland, Oregon: Timber Press. 2017.

Oudolf, Piet and Noël Kingsbury. *Designing with Plants*. Portland, Oregon: Timber Press. 2000.

Oudolf, Piet and and Noël Kingsbury. *Planting Design: Gardens in Time and Space*. Portland, Oregon. Timber Press. 2005.

Pearson, Dan. *Garden Inspiration*. London. Murray & Sorrell FUEL. 2009.

Richardson, Tim. *The Arcadian Friends: Inventing the English Landscape Garden*. London: Bantam Press. 2008.

Richardson, Tim. 'Psychotopia' in *Vista: The Culture and Politics of Gardens*. London. Frances Lincoln. 2005.

Rocca, Allesandro (ed.). *Planetary Gardens: The Landscape Architecture of Gilles Clément*. Basel, Switzerland: Birkhäuser Verlag AG. 2008.

Rainer, Thomas and Claudia West. *Planting in a Post-Wild World: Designing Plant Communities for Resilient Landscapes*. Portland, Oregon: Timber Press. 2015.

Stevens, Wallace. *The Collected Poems*. New York: Alfred A. Knopf. 2008.

Stuart, Rory. *What Are Gardens For?* London: Frances Lincoln Limited. 2012.

Stuart-Smith, Tom. 'Space and Enclosure', a talk given at The Garden Museum Literary Festival, Petworth House, UK. 2013. https://vimeo.com/108992173

Van Valkenburgh, Michael. *Designing a Garden: The Monk's Garden at the Isabella Stewart Gardener Museum*. New York: The Monacelli Press. 2019.

ABOUT THE AUTHOR

James Golden, born in Mississippi though resident in New York City for most of his life, was a writer in the corporate world. Nearing retirement, and embarking on what he happily calls *la vita nuova*, he acquired a property in western New Jersey to make a garden. It was an unusual site for a garden—little more than a clearing in a wood on heavy, wet clay—but he was taken with the site's emotional power and the intangible qualities of the landscape. Fifteen years on, James is a celebrated garden maker and thinker whose garden, Federal Twist, has featured in numerous publications including *The New York Times*, *Gardens Illustrated*, *Horticulture*, and several other magazines and books. Monty Don visited Federal Twist in 2019 for the BBC Gardener's World series *American Gardens* and described it as 'a magical, superlative garden'. James has written for the *Garden Design Journal* and is known for his thoughtful commentary and design. He has been a garden blogger for 15 years at federaltwist.com and lectures for a variety of institutions and groups. He is a member and participant in the Garden Conservancy's Open Days program, the American Horticultural Society, the New York Botanical Garden, the Brooklyn Botanical Garden, the Ecological Landscape Alliance, and the Pennsylvania Horticultural Society.

Follow the story of Federal Twist:
@imfederaltwist
federaltwist.com
federaltwistdesign.org

PRAISE FOR FEDERAL TWIST

'The entire garden flows out of a profound acceptance of what exists as a way of creating something utterly new and expressive.'
'It challenges one's perception of what a garden is.'
THOMAS RAINER AND CLAUDIA WEST, *Planting in a Post-Wild World*

'Everything about Federal Twist simultaneously challenges and breaks every rule while sinuously obeying the laws of plants and how they can grow. This takes great expertise, patience—and the willingness to fail.
MONTY DON, *American Gardens*

'More than magic was needed to garden on this challenging site; alchemy, or turning a leaden site golden, was what he accomplished.'
CHRISTOPHER WOODS, *Garden Lust*

'What a truly 21st-century garden this is.'
NOEL KINGSBURY *Gardens Illustrated* magazine

The garden opens regularly to garden tour groups such as those from the Garden Conservancy, the Pennsylvania Horticultural Society, the Hardy Plant Society, as well as to private tours.

For more information, please contact James Golden at federaltwistroad@gmail.com

ACKNOWLEDGEMENTS

I say somewhere in this book that I'm a 'book gardener'. And I doubt this book would have come into existence if I hadn't suddenly come upon several astonishing books in the early 2000's by a group of garden designers, writers and thinkers associated with what we have come to call the new perennial movement—Piet Oudolf, Noel Kingsbury, Henk Gerritsen chief among them. These books caught my attention, and gave me a vision. I learned from them.

Thanks to the Germans—Karl Foerster, Hans Pagels, Richard Hansen, Cassian Schmidt and others—whose work I would learn of largely through the writings of Noel Kingsbury. The world of gardens is a rather magical place where wonderful and unexpected things happen. In uncovering the history of new perennials, Noel became the purveyor of a long history of German plant and gardening research and practice that was, to my knowledge, available nowhere else in the English language—knowledge that paved the way for the naturalistic garden movement of today. I want thank all of these people (some unnamed, I'm sure).

I first 'met' Thomas Rainer on my blog many years ago. Thomas had his own blog, and we exchanged quite a few comments and ideas in the early days. Though he probably didn't know it, Thomas became a kind of mentor and guide, and an important American link into a horticultural world that seemed very Europe-centered to me. Thank you, Thomas, for your early example and encouragement, and thank you for writing the foreword to this book.

I'm extraordinarily grateful to Anna Mumford, my publisher and editor, who gave me this opportunity to publish, and whose guidance and advice helped shape this book. It wouldn't have happened without her knowledge and acute attention to turning my sometimes less-than-ordered process of thinking into a book.

I also owe a world of gratitude to Giacomo Guzzon, a landscape architect living in London. We met almost by accident in London in 2015 and became close friends, visited gardens together in the US and Europe, and talked endlessly about plants and gardens. Giacomo read parts of my manuscript and, more importantly, talked through ideas and concepts with me during the writing of this book. I'm sure he will recognize more than a few ideas we've endlessly discussed.

Another person without whom my garden would not exist is Milton Najera, my gardener since the beginning. Milton, at first with his father, Ernesto, then alone, built the stone walls, planted the plants, dug the ponds, made the gravel paths, and continues to care for the garden. I owe him a special debt of gratitude.

I dedicate this book to my life partner, now husband, Phillip Saperia. Without him, there would be no house, no garden, no life within a garden.

INDEX

INDEX

First published in 2021 by Filbert Press
filbertpress.com

Text and photographs © 2021 James Golden
FRONT COVER IMAGE Claire Takacs
GARDEN MAPS AND DRAWINGS Carl Molter and Giacomo Guzzon
BOOK DESIGN Michael Whitehead

Thanks to the publishers for permission to quote material from the following works:
The Collected Poems, Wallace Stevens, Penguin Random House.
Planting in a Post-Wild World © by Thomas Rainer and Claudia West. Published by Timber Press,
Portland, OR. Used by permission of the publisher. All rights reserved.
Planetary Gardens: The Landscape Architecture of Gilles Clément, Allesandro Rocca, (ed).
Birkhäuser Verlag AG., Basel, Switzerland.

The typefaces used in the book are Adobe Caslon (serif) and Berthold Akzidenz Grotesk
(sans serif). The ligatures seen in the introductory quotes to each chapter reference the
earliest forms of writing when scribes found that combining letters speeded up the process
of written communication. Here they are used purely decoratively.

A catalogue record for this book is available from the British Library
ISBN: 978-1-9997345-7-2

10 9 8 7 6 5 4 3 2   22 23 24 25 26 27 28 29

Printed by Printer Trento S.r.l., Italy